ULTIMATE
Cross Stitch
PROJECTS

W9-AKC-104

ULTIMATE
Cross Stitch
COLORFUL AND INSPIRING
DESIGNS FROM MARIA DIAZ
PROJECTS

Maria Diaz

CROSS STITCH
Collection

Ultimate Cross Stitch Projects is an original work, first published in 2011 in the United Kingdom by Future Publishing Limited in magazine form under the title *The Ultimate Maria Diaz Collection*. This title is printed and distributed in North America under license. All rights reserved.

ISBN 978-1-57421-444-4

© 2013 by Design Originals, www.d-originals.com, an imprint of Fox Chapel Publishing, 800-457-9112, 1970 Broad Street, East Petersburg, PA 17520.

Printed in China
First printing

Contents

You'll find inspiration on every page of this amazing collection of cross stitch designs

Florals

Bring a burst of color and spring freshness into your home

Baby

Four timeless designs that capture all the wonder of a new life

Art

Exquisite paintings transformed into cross stitch for you

Welcome!

to the Ultimate Cross Stitch Collection of Maria Diaz! This unique book brings together an incredible set of designs from this well-known cross stitch artist. Maria's designs have a wide appeal—from stunning flowers and landscapes to animals and much loved baby pictures, there's something to stitch for everyone. You'll be inspired by her clever use of color, from the bright, bold images like the Poppy (page 78) to the peaceful feel of her sepia images like the Madonna and Child (page 124). Whatever stunning design you choose to start with, you'll turn to this book again and again for years of stitching pleasure.

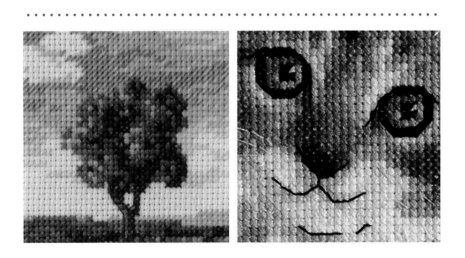

MEET THE DESIGNER...
Maria Diaz

Life-long lover of crafts, Maria Diaz, speaks to the Editors of Cross Stitch Collection about what inspires her to create such beautiful designs...

Maria has recently enjoyed her 20th year as a needlecraft designer, and to celebrate her successes, we explore her career so far, from the first tentative steps as a silk screen printer to today's universally acclaimed fame.

What's your background, and how did you come to be a cross stitch designer?

I have always enjoyed craft and making things, ever since I can remember. My grandmother was a dressmaker and she taught me how to sew and embroider as a child. (My great-grandmother taught me how to play cards—she was a barmaid!) Being artistically driven, although not particularly academic, I was determined to go to Art school and grow up to be hugely famous, producing works of great importance from a New York loft apartment! I went to study in Leicester, and while I was there, I got a holiday job silk screen printing at the DMC factory. One thing led to another, and before long I was designing embroideries and learning to chart cross stitch patterns. On graduating, I was offered a full-time position, becoming their first in-house designer. I loved working with the team at DMC, it was a real family atmosphere and my skills were nurtured. After working for the company for eight years, I was managing the design and development department. Although I still loved my job, it was becoming less creative and more managerial. I felt it was time to see what I could do on my own, so I moved back to London, went freelance and fortunately landed a position as a specialist consultant on a needlecraft project—I soon started gaining regular monthly magazine commissions. The rest, as they say, is history.

What inspires your designs?

When given the seed of an idea, I really enjoy researching a project and tend to create a pictorial

This light and spacious studio was purpose built for Maria and her designs after many years spent cramped in the box room at home!

"I really enjoy researching a project and tend to create a pictorial story in my head..."

story in my head, especially when working on figurative or animal pieces. I like to give character to them, bringing them to life a little. I'm a huge fan of Art Nouveau, especially the work of Alphonse Mucha. Often, the style of his paintings can be seen reflected in my designs.

The flower studies require a slightly different approach. With these, the colors, shapes and wonder of nature draw me in. Often, it is those designs that I really struggle with at the beginning, which turn out to be the most successful by the end.

This beautiful and intricate embellishment on her wedding dress epitomizes Maria's love of and dedication to crafts.

Maria transforms iconic artwork into cross stitch masterpieces.

What process does your work go through to transform from an idea to an actual design?

I used to spend a lot of time at the library, but in our computer age, there is a wealth of knowledge at your fingertips at home, which makes research so easy. I tend to sketch out my idea first, putting a rough outline on paper and sometimes I add shading. Then I scan the sketch and import it onto my specialist design software package, which effectively enables me to trace over my sketch in stitches. I do all my color work stitch by stitch on screen—I suppose it's similar to painting by numbers!

Where do you work? Describe your studio.

After years of working in the box room, or on the dining table, we eventually borrowed from the bank and built a garage at the end of our garden, a portion of which we converted into an amazing studio. It is large and bright and can accommodate all my junk! After I drop the boys at school, I make a cuppa and then head to work. I like to listen to the radio as I work—it keeps me in touch with the outside world. Funnily, I have to put alarms on my phone to remind me to collect the boys, as I can get so absorbed in my work that I lose all track of time!

"One of the most rewarding things I have found is how others put their own slant on your patterns"

How does it feel seeing your designs being stitched by people the world over?

It is wonderfully encouraging to know that people enjoy what I do. I have spoken to people at exhibitions and been very humbled by their thanks and appreciation. It is lovely when people ask after my family; it always surprises me that I am so well known, and I suppose, in a small way, I have realized my dream of being famous.

Design-wise, have you got anything exciting planned for the future?

Now that would be telling!

What are your top tips for budding cross stitch designers?

Perseverance is key. You have to enjoy the process from start to finish, and don't be too precious about your designs. One of the most rewarding things I have found is how others put their own slant on your patterns by changing the color of threads or adding beads. Once I have finished my process, the design then starts its own life, and evolves in the hands of other stitchers.

Alphonse Mucha painted 'Dance' in 1898. This romantic Art Nouveau piece is Maria's favorite painting. Mucha's influences can be seen in so much of her cross stitch work.

Animals

Whether it's feathers or fur that you love,
Maria's got it covered—with designs to make
a charming companion for every season

The kitten's delightful expression is crucial, and it's achieved with backstitch details like the whisker and the white glints in its eyes

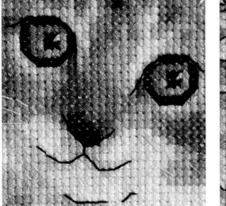 

Petals and purrs

Frolic among the gorgeous rose blooms with this adorable kitten. He's ready to bring life and fun to your home!

Maria has captured the glint in this kitten's eyes wonderfully—you can see he's full of life and going to be into mischief at any second. The bright blue eyes and soft fur coat make this adorable kitten irresistible to stitch, too. The subtle color changes in the piece make the kitten and roses appear marvellously realistic. The design itself is easy to stitch, as only a few fractionals are worked to shape the eyes. The combination of simple stitching techniques and bold colors make this an enjoyable project to complete. ➤

➤ Stitching your kitten

To stitch your design, you will need to find the center of a piece of 16x14in (41x36cm) aida so fold the fabric in half and then into quarters. The center is where the points meet. Work this design using two strands of cotton over one aida block. If you are using an evenweave fabric, the stitches are worked over two threads. Cross stitch from the center of your fabric and chart, working outwards across the design.

Beautiful shading

A beautiful palette of creams and browns has been used to create a lifelike appearance to the kitten's fur. Try to work in good light to help distinguish between shades of the pink roses. As this project will take some time, try to avoid leaving your needles in the fabric because needles can leave rust spots, which are very difficult to remove. If possible, it is also a good idea to take your fabric out of the frame when you are not working, as the fabric can stretch. If you are a little short of time, the background area in this design can be worked in half cross stitch. This is quicker to work and will give a more subtle look to the background.

Picture details

Backstitch is used to define the shapes of the roses and create a textured look for the kitten's fur and whiskers. The backstitch is simple, but you may want to work the whiskers in longer stitches to make them more noticeable.

Shopping list...

- ✦ 14ct aida, 16x14in (41x36cm), white (or 28ct evenweave)
- ✦ Embroidery floss, as listed in the key
- ✦ Frame, with a 10x8in (25x20cm) aperture, wood

Petals and purrs

	DMC	Anchor	Madeira	Color
Cross stitch in two strands				
·|·	White	002	2402	White
♡|♡	151	074	0607	Light pink
▲|▲	160	939	0906	Dark blue
I|I	453	231	1806	Grey
J|J	644	391	1814	Light stone
ı|ı	712	926	2101	Cream
+|+	818	023	0502	V light pink
~|~	822	390	1908	V lt stone
ƨ|ƨ	841	1082	2002	Mink
◇|◇	950	4146	2309	Flesh
∩|∩	989	242	1401	Light green
◪|◪	3031	905	2003	M brown
|	3348	264	1409	V lt green
⋈|⋈	3362	263	2603	Dark green
℈|℈	3363	262	1602	M green
■|■	3371	382	2004	Dk brown
◉|◉	3731	076	0506	Dark pink
♥|♥	3733	075	0504	Med pink
▲|▲	3752	1032	1002	Med blue
◿|◿	3756	1037	2504	Light blue
×|×	3782	388	1906	Med stone
□|□	3790	904	1905	Dark stone
●|●	3803	069	2609	V dk pink
O|O	3861	233	1807	Purple grey
#|#	3863	378	1911	Lt brown

	DMC	Anchor	Madeira	Color
Backstitch in one strand				
——	*White	002	2402	White
whiskers				
——	*3371	382	2004	Dk brown
all other outlines and details				

Stitched using DMC threads on 14ct aida

Stitch count 140x112

Design area 10x8in (25x20cm)

*indicates color is listed earlier in the key

The cat's stunning green eyes are offset by the holly leaves. The little details like the color matching and backstitch whiskers bring the cat to life

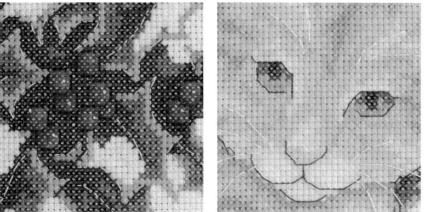

Holly
& whiskers

Create this playful kitten amongst the holly and give a fellow feline lover the most purrfect Christmas present!

This endearing picture of a cat playing among the Christmas decorations was inspired by Maria's own experience. She says, "My sister-in-law had a new kitten last year, and we came home after an evening out to find the Christmas tree, plus all the baubles and lights, scattered over the living room floor!" ➤

➤ Get stitching

The delicate details and depth of shading make this cat appear wonderfully lifelike. You may even like to change the color of the fur to resemble your own pet. You can easily select alternative thread colors using an embroidery floss shade card. Details unique to your cat could be included in your design, such as a white paw.

Before you start stitching, it is a good idea to prepare your fabric. The first step is to check for any marks or stains. If your fabric is new, then this is unlikely to be a problem, but if the fabric has been stored in damp conditions or direct sunlight, you will need to check for mold and color fading. Start by pressing the fabric to remove any creases, and then oversew the edges to prevent them from fraying. Aida is less likely to fray compared with evenweave, but the raw edges can catch your thread as you work. Before you start stitching, it is always advisable to check that your fabric is large enough to accommodate the whole design, and allow excess fabric for framing. We tend to allow an extra 3in (8cm) around each design in our shopping list (above left).

Stitching your design

To stitch your design, you will need to find the center of the fabric. You can do this simply by folding the fabric in half and then into quarters. Cross stitch from the middle point to place the design centrally. Work the cross stitch using two strands over one aida block. You can help to keep track of stitched areas by marking your chart with a highlighter pen. However, it is advisable to keep the pen to one side when marking the chart, as it may stain your fabric if accidently dropped. To help reference the chart as you work, try adding tacking stitches every ten holes in the fabric. The stitches can then be removed as the design develops.

Adding the details

A pearlescent DMC Light Effects thread is used in the design to make small patches of the snow glisten—as if the winter sunshine is bouncing off the snow underfoot. If you wanted to add a bit more sparkle to the remaining areas of snow, try blending one strand of pearlescent thread with one strand of white cotton. Once the cross stitch is done, add the backstitch using one strand. You can keep the backstitch neat by keeping an even stitching tension as you work.

Holly & whiskers

	DMC	Anchor	Madeira	Color
Cross stitch in two strands				
·|·	White	002	2402	White (2)
⋈⋈	319	1044	1313	V dark green
♡♡	321	047	0510	Medium red
◇◇	367	216	1312	Dark green
⌐⌐	368	214	1310	Medium green
✕✕	415	398	1802	Dark grey
#|#	435	365	2010	Very dark tan
⧖⧖	436	363	2011	Dark tan
&|&	437	362	2012	Medium tan
ⱱ|ⱱ	522	860	1513	Moss green
⋒⋒	666	046	0210	Light red
⊤⊤	712	926	2101	Light cream
2|2	738	361	2013	Light tan
~|~	739	366	2014	Dark cream
⊥⊥	754	1012	0305	Light peach
ɜ|ɜ	758	9575	2309	Dark peach
⁄⁄	762	234	1804	Light grey
▸▸	801	359	2007	Brown
♥♥	815	044	0513	Dark red
◆◆	986	246	1404	Bright green
▦▦	3799	236	1713	Charcoal
✶✶	DMC E5200 Light Effects			

	DMC	Anchor	Madeira	Color
Backstitch in one strand				
—	*White	002	2402	White
ears, whiskers				
—	369	1043	1309	Light green
holly leaves				
—	*801	359	2007	Brown
cat details				
—	*3799	236	1713	Charcoal
berries				

	DMC	Anchor	Madeira	Color
French knots in one strand				
●●	*White	002	2402	White
berries				

Stitched using DMC threads on 14ct aida
Stitch count 139×112, Design area 10×8in (25×20cm)
*indicates color is listed earlier in the key
(2) indicates more than one skein required

The duck has **lots of interesting details to stitch and you may want to use a French knot for its eye**

River birds

Take a trip down to the river to see these familiar birds, beautifully created in cross stitch for you

This riverside scene is wonderfully tranquil and makes a great companion piece to the garden birds featured on p.27. In both designs, the birds are beautifully represented to make them very lifelike. Maria has plenty of memories to draw on for inspiration, "I used to live in a cottage next to a canal" she explained, "the ducks and swans would come right up to my door to be fed!"

➤

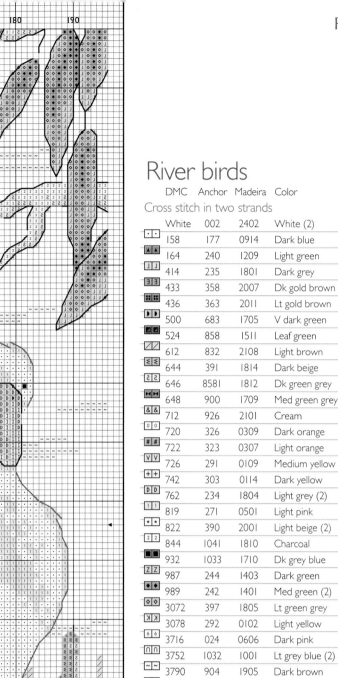

River birds

	DMC	Anchor	Madeira	Color
Cross stitch in two strands				
	White	002	2402	White (2)
⊡⊡	158	177	0914	Dark blue
▲▲	164	240	1209	Light green
JJ	414	235	1801	Dark grey
33	433	358	2007	Dk gold brown
⊞⊞	436	363	2011	Lt gold brown
▶▶	500	683	1705	V dark green
▨▨	524	858	1511	Leaf green
⧄⧄	612	832	2108	Light brown
⧩⧩	644	391	1814	Dark beige
22	646	8581	1812	Dk green grey
⋈⋈	648	900	1709	Med green grey
&&&	712	926	2101	Cream
00	720	326	0309	Dark orange
##	722	323	0307	Light orange
VV	726	291	0109	Medium yellow
++	742	303	0114	Dark yellow
DD	762	234	1804	Light grey (2)
II	819	271	0501	Light pink
⊡⊡	822	390	2001	Light beige (2)
22	844	1041	1810	Charcoal
■■	932	1033	1710	Dk grey blue
ZZ	987	244	1403	Dark green
◆◆	989	242	1401	Med green (2)
◌◌	3072	397	1805	Lt green grey
KK	3078	292	0102	Light yellow
⋂⋂	3716	024	0606	Dark pink
⋂⋂	3752	1032	1001	Lt grey blue (2)
~~	3790	904	1905	Dark brown
●●	3839	176	2702	Light blue
▲▲	3844	433	1103	Bright blue
＝＝	3855	311	0113	Apricot
⊞⊞				

Backstitch in one strand

—	*414	235	1801	Dark grey
	dragonfly, goose, heron, swans			
▬	*844	1041	1810	Charcoal
	all other outlines and details			

French knots in one strand

●●	*844	1041	1810	Charcoal
	dragonfly			

Stitched using DMC threads on 28ct evenweave
over two threads

Stitch count 168x196

Design area 12x14in (31x36cm)

*indicates color is listed earlier in the key

(2) indicates more than one skein required

Animals

Animals

➤ Getting started

This peaceful scene of riverside birds is simply beautiful, and it will look great hung in any room of the house. The natural colors and subtle shading make the birds appear so realistic. We have stitched this design on to a pale blue evenweave to give a soft, water-like appearance to the unstitched areas. When using an evenweave or linen fabric, it is a good idea to over sew the edges. This prevents the edges from fraying as you work. As there are gaps between stitched areas, you will need to count the threads to place certain elements of the design. You may find it useful to work tacking stitches every 20 threads as guidelines to mark 10x10 stitches on the chart. Work from the center of your fabric using two strands over two threads of evenweave. You can help keep your stitches looking neat by letting your needle hang freely to unwind now and then. Any twists in threads can give an unwanted uneven appearance to your stitching.

Alternative fabric

The pale blue evenweave depicts the water in the design, but you may wish to use a different color background in your piece. If you are planning to stitch on to a white background, you could work the water ripples in lighter shades of turquoise or blue to create a similar effect.

Backstitch details

The backstitch draws in all the lovely little details in this design, defining the birds' features and adding texture to bring the piece to life. Work the backstitch using one strand of cotton in your needle. The French knot details on the dragonfly are also worked using one strand. Work the French knots by wrapping one strand of cotton twice around your needle. Now take your needle back through the fabric and gently pull the thread to create a neat knot.

This design is full of character! Each bird has its own personality and would make a lovely piece individually. But shown all together as a group, combined with the calming collection of colors and expressive detailing, this picture is irresistible!

Chirpy visitors

Stitch these four fabulous bird designs. They make great cards, or they can be combined together as a single framed piece to celebrate our garden visitors

Shopping list...

- ✦ **14ct aida**, 7x7in (18x18cm) per card, white (or 28ct evenweave)
- ✦ **Embroidery floss**, as listed in the key
- ✦ **Cards**, round aperture, pale yellow and lavender
- ✦ **Cards**, square aperture, pale yellow and lavender

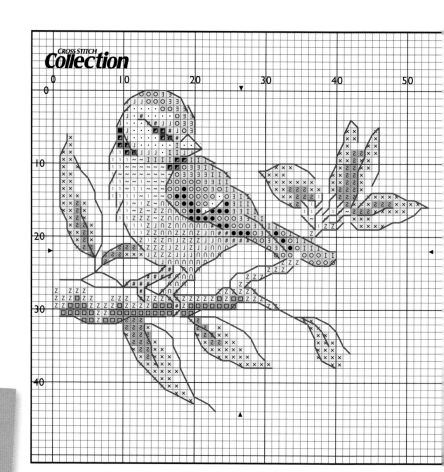

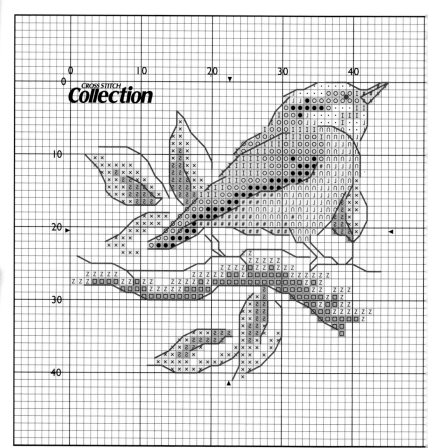

Chirpy visitors

	DMC	Anchor	Madeira	Color
Cross stitch in two strands				
·I·	White	002	2402	White
III	159	120	0901	Mauve
22	320	215	1311	Dark green
xx	368	214	1310	Light green
◆◆	407	914	2312	Dark flesh
■■	535	401	1809	Very dark grey
∩∩	644	391	1814	Light stone
▨▨	646	8581	1812	Dark grey
##	648	900	1813	Medium grey
~~	726	295	0109	Medium yellow
++	742	303	0114	Dark yellow
♡♡	758	9575	0403	Light peach
33	813	161	1013	Blue
OO	932	1033	1710	Light grey blue
◇◇	950	4146	2309	Light flesh
·*·	963	023	0503	Pink
□□	3022	1040	1903	Dark stone
JJ	3024	397	1901	Light grey
ꞁꞁ	3078	292	0102	Light yellow
◕◕	3768	779	2508	Dark grey blue
♥♥	3778	1013	0402	Dark peach
ZZ	3782	388	1906	Beige

Backstitch in one strand

——	*535	401	1809	Very dark grey
	all outlines and details			

French knots in one strand

●●	*535	401	1809	Very dark grey
	eyes			

Stitched using DMC threads on 14ct aida

Maximum stitch count 51x54

Design area 3¾x3¾in (9x10cm)

*indicates color is listed earlier in the key

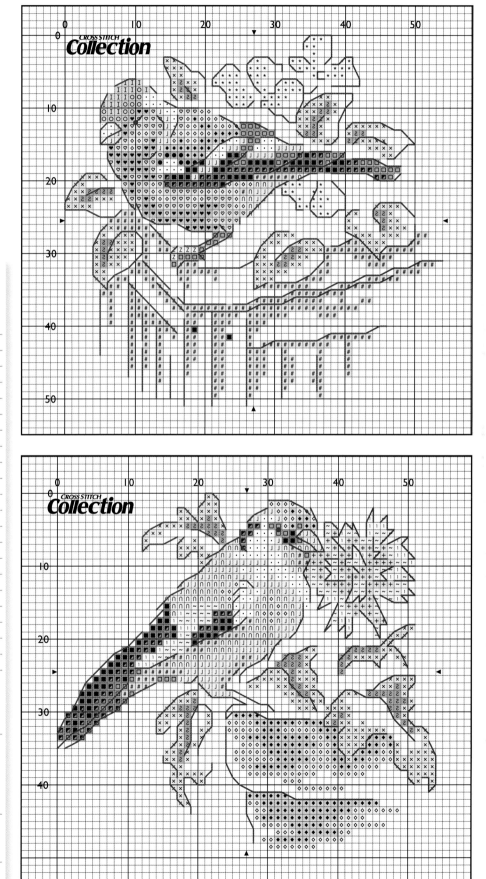

Shopping list...

- ✦ 28ct evenweave, 15×16in (38×41cm), white (or 14ct aida)
- ✦ Embroidery floss, as listed in the key
- ✦ Frame, with a 9½×10in (24×25cm) aperture

➤ Start stitching

This winter scene is magnificently lifelike and a real delight to stitch. The freshly fallen snow glistens with metallic threads and the bright markings of the birds look so striking. Start stitching your design by finding the center of your fabric. Work outwards from this point to place your design centrally. Cross stitch using two strands of cotton over two threads of the evenweave fabric.

Perfect backstitch

The backstitch details give the design its rustic charm and make the birds appear so realistic. Try working the backstitch using a slightly smaller needle. If you have worked the design using a size 24 tapestry needle, change to a size 26 when working the backstitch. The smaller needle will slip between worked areas and your stitches will have a neater finish as a result.

Technical tips

It is a good idea to wash your hands before stitching, particularly when working with light threads, as they can be discolored. If your work becomes a little dull, which white fabrics like this one easily do, then try giving it a spring clean by gently washing your stitching in a mild detergent. Once dry, place your stitching face down on a clean towel and press with a medium heat.

Feathered friends

	DMC	Anchor	Madeira	Color
Cross stitch in two strands				
·|·	White	002	2402	White
■■	310	403	2400	Black
♡♡	349	013	0212	Light red
◆◆	413	236	1713	V dark grey
▲▲	414	235	1801	Dark grey
△△	415	398	1802	Medium grey
⋉⋊	422	372	2102	Med straw
DD	436	363	2011	Tan
♥♥	498	1005	0511	Dark red
ZZ	522	860	1513	Dark green
⋜⋜	612	832	2108	Dark straw
⊹⊹⊹	644	391	1814	L grey brown
II	712	926	2101	Light cream
nn	721	324	0308	Orange
⊿⊿	739	366	2014	Dark cream
++	742	303	0114	Dark yellow
JJ	744	301	0112	Light yellow
22	762	234	1804	Light grey
77	926	850	1707	Green grey
●●	3031	905	2003	Dark brown
33	3032	898	2002	D grey brown
⋈⋈	3047	852	2205	Light straw

	DMC	Anchor	Madeira	Color
Cross stitch in two strands				
VV	3053	843	1510	Light green
22	3747	120	0901	Blue
~~	3756	1037	2504	Ice blue (2)
III	3782	388	1906	Light brown
＃＃	3790	904	1905	Med brown
▷▷	3862	944	2106	Gold brown
★★	E5200			Light Effects

Backstitch in one strand

—	*White	002	2402	White
	eyes			
—	*414	235	1801	Dark grey
	snow			
—	*3031	905	2003	Dark brown
	all other outlines and details			

Stitched using DMC threads on 28ct evenweave over two threads

Stitch count 132×136

Design area 9¼×9¾in (24×25cm)

*indicates color is listed earlier in the key

(2) indicates more than one skein required

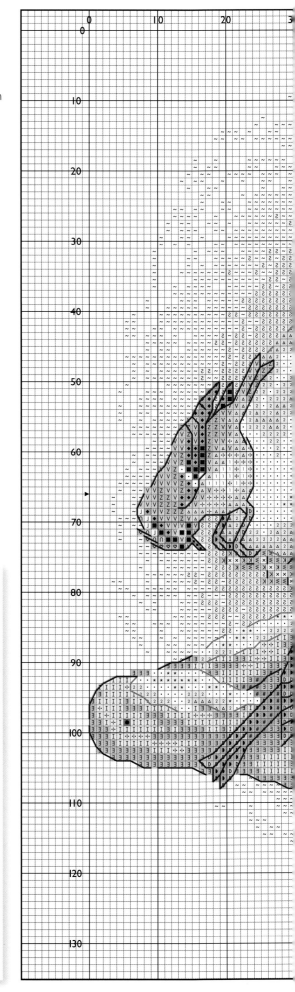

The piglets' true to life colors, and the bold florals that surround their inquisitive faces, are what make this design so striking

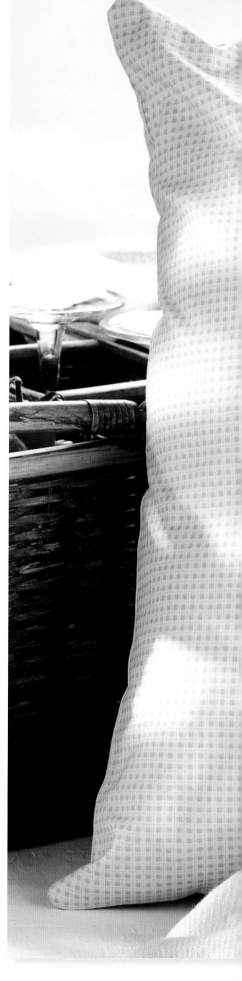

Two little pigs

Aren't these adorable piglets just irresistible? You will love making every stitch as you create this happy scene

Maria has created a design full of character and life; these pretty piglets are bound to bring a smile to your face. These cheeky chaps are surrounded by beautiful spring flowers—you certainly don't need to have spent time in the country to appreciate this inspiring piece! The piglets seem to have taken on a character all of their own, and whether you make this up into a cushion or a framed picture, it's a pig perfect design to stitch. ➤

➤ Organizing your threads

There are quite a lot of close shades of the same color in this design, so you will find it easier if you make a thread organizer before you start stitching. Take a piece of thin card and punch 29 holes in it, as that's how many different colors of thread there are. Next to each hole, write down the color number, name and the chart symbol used to identify it. Now

Two little pigs

	DMC	Anchor	Madeira	Color
Cross stitch in two strands				
★★	208	110	0804	Dark purple
✰✰	209	109	0711	Medium purple
⋆⋆	211	342	0801	Light purple
●●	319	1044	1313	Very dark green
@@	320	215	1311	Medium green
▲▲	340	118	0902	Dark heather
△△	341	117	0901	Light heather
◆◆	367	216	1312	Dark green
⊙⊙	368	214	1310	Light green
○○	369	1043	1309	Very light green
ƧƧ	437	362	2011	Dark sand
◇◇	603	055	0701	Medium pink
22	605	1094	0613	Light pink
⁄⁄	738	361	2013	Light sand
33	743	297	0113	Yellow
++	828	9159	1014	Blue
##	840	1084	1912	Dark stone
××	841	1082	1911	Medium stone
□□	842	1080	1910	Light stone
11	950	4146	2309	Light flesh
ℨℨ	961	076	0610	Dark pink
♡♡	3064	914	2312	Medium flesh
·∶·	3770	1009	2314	Peach
♥♥	3772	1007	2310	Dark flesh
~~	3774	778	0306	Very light flesh
⋈⋈	3787	1041	1811	Olive green
◆◆	3803	069	2609	Very dark pink
✕✕	3854	1002	2513	Orange
Backstitch in one strand				
——	632	936	2311	Very dark flesh
	piglet outlines		
——	*3787	904	1811	Olive green
	piglet eyes and nostrils, fence outlines and birds		
——	*3803	069	2609	Very dark pink
	flower outlines		

Stitched using DMC threads on 14ct aida
Stitch count 113x139
Design area 8x10in (21x25cm)

*indicates color is listed earlier in the key

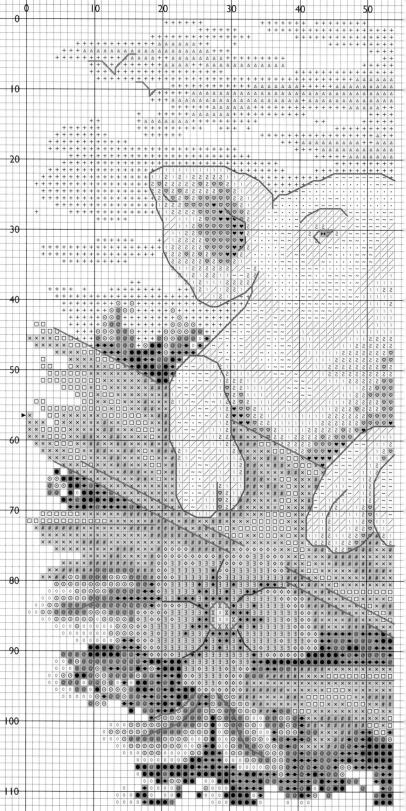

loop each color through the corresponding hole. You will now easily be able to find the correct color at a glance. When you have used more than half of a skein, the labels tend to slip off and you can't identify what the color number is. By organizing your threads in this way any left over thread you have can easily be used for another cross stitch project.

Stitching the design

All the cross stitch is worked in two strands of embroidery floss over one thread of the aida fabric. When you have worked all the cross stitch, you can add the backstitch details: Very dark flesh for the piglet outlines; Olive green for the piglet eyes and nostrils, fence outlines and birds; and Very dark pink for the flower outlines.

The snowy background is left largely unstitched, so it comes together very quickly as you work it. Backstitch is essential for bringing the snowdrops to life

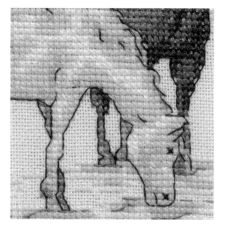 

Crisp
winter morning

Bring this evocative country scene to life and take time to enjoy the beauty of the horses, crocuses and snowdrops in winter

The world always looks like a completely different place when there's snow on the ground, and this unusual landscape can create stunning scenes of natural beauty, just like this one! Maria is well-known for her ability to successfully capture animals in cross stitch, and she has done a marvellous job here. She explains the effect she was after, "I have tried to capture the cold, crisp feel of a winter morning. The horses would usually be wearing blankets with it being that cold, but I have kept the picture as featuring just the natural elements." ➤

- ✦ 28ct evenweave, 16×16in (41×41cm)
- ✦ Embroidery floss, as listed in the key
- ✦ Burlap, 25×50in (63×127cm)
- ✦ Lining fabric, 25×50in (63×127cm) to coordinate
- ✦ Piping cord, 50in (172cm) thick cord

➤ Stitching the design

Fold your fabric in half both ways to find the center as this is the best place to start stitching. Follow the arrows on the sides of the chart to find the corresponding position. All the cross stitch is worked in two strands of embroidery floss over two threads of the evenweave fabric. All of the leaves in the background and the nut are worked in half cross stitch in two strands. Make sure that all these stitches point in the same direction.

Adding the details

When you have worked all the cross stitch, you can add the backstitch details. These are worked in one strand: Straw for the nut outline, leaves, ears and tail details and Dark brown for all other outlines and details.

Autumn gatherer

	DMC	Anchor	Madeira	Color
Cross stitch in two strands				
★★	434	310	2009	Dark golden brown
☆☆	435	365	2010	Mid golden brown
★✱	436	363	2011	Light golden brown
◻◻	437	362	2012	Tan
♥♥	632	936	2311	Dark sepia
2 2	712	926	2101	Light cream
3 3	738	361	2013	Dark cream
▲▲	739	366	2014	Medium cream
##	839	1086	1913	Medium brown
~~	977	1002	2301	Orange
♡♡	3064	914	2312	Light sepia
◼◼	3371	382	2004	Dark brown
@@	3772	1007	2601	Medium sepia
✗✗	3862	358	1912	Light brown
Half cross stitch in two strands				
╱╱	422	372	2102	Medium sand
++	676	891	2208	Light sand
2 2	3045	888	2103	Dark sand
Backstitch in one strand				
──	3047	852	2205	Straw
	nut outline and leaves, ears and tail details			
──	*3371	382	2004	Dark brown
	all other outlines and details			

Stitched using DMC threads on 28ct evenweave over two threads

Stitch count 112×112

Design area 8×8in (20×20cm)

*indicates color is listed earlier in the key

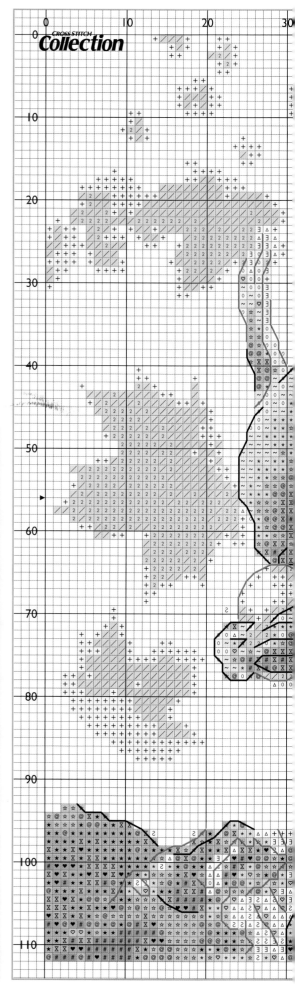

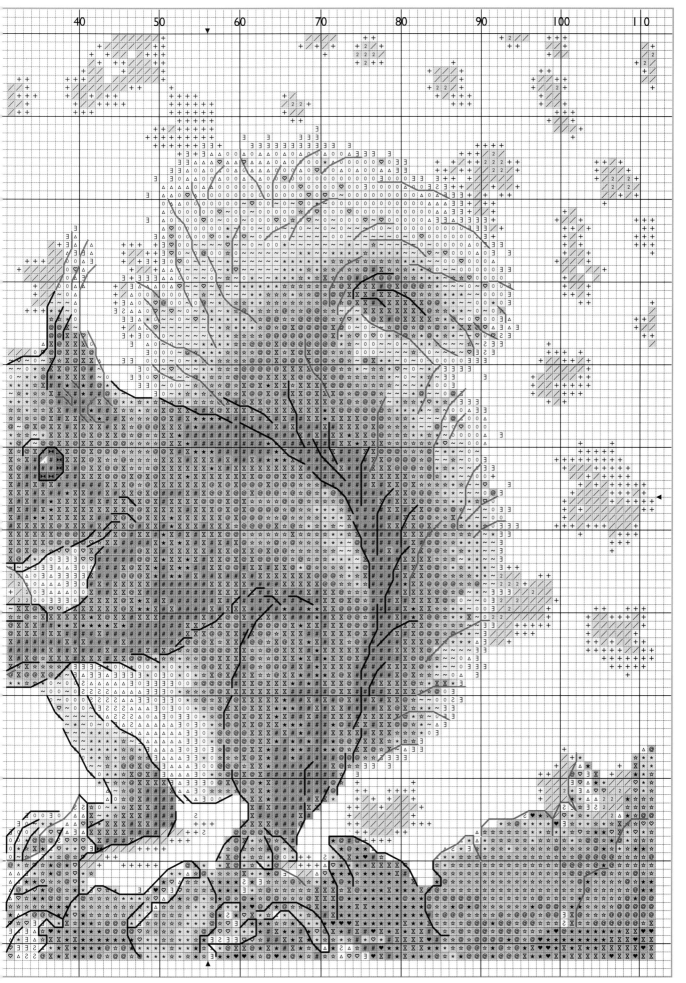

Extras for you...

Get more from your stitching with these extra projects to make...

Gather up your own autumn harvest by making this terrific bag as well

Making the **bag**

1. Cut the burlap (see box below) into the following pieces:
   Bag front and back; two pieces 16x16in (41x41cm)
   Bag gusset; 5x50in (13x127cm)
   Bag handles; two pieces 2½x25in (6x63cm)
   Lining front and back; two pieces 16x16in (41x41cm)
   Lining gusset; 5x50in (13x127cm)

2. Trim the stitched evenweave to 1in (2.5cm) outside the outer edge of the stitching all the way round. Turn the edges under ½in (1.5cm), then pin to the center of the bag front. Machine stitch into place.

3. Use a ½in (1.5cm) seam allowance throughout and press all seams open as you go.

4. Place the bag gusset and the bag front right sides together and stitch down one side, along the bottom and up the other side. Attach the bag back to the other side of the bag gusset.

5. Repeat this stage with the lining front, gusset and back.

6. Take one of the handle strips and turn the long edges over ½in (1.5cm) to the wrong side, then fold the strip in half lengthways to enclose the folded-under edges. Stitch together close to the edge.

7. Cut the piping cord in half and thread it through the handle to give it strength. Repeat with the other handle.

Working with... **Burlap**

Many supermarkets are selling jute fiber bags as a green alternative to plastic carrier bags. You can either attach your finished cross stitch to one of these, or make your own. This one is made from burlap, which is easily available in fabric stores. It is made from fine jute or flax, and is similar to standard hessian, except that it has a tighter and more regular weave. It's a very wide fabric, usually 72in (180cm).

8. Pin one of the bag handles to the top of the front of the bag, positioning each end 4in (10cm) from the side seam and matching the raw edges. Pin the other handle to the back of the bag in the same place.

9. Now place the bag outer and bag lining right sides together by turning the lining inside out and placing the bag outer inside it. Stitch together round the top enclosing the handles and leave a 3in (8cm) opening along one side.

10. Turn right sides out, press and stitch along the top of the bag, close to the edge to neaten, and stitch the opening closed to complete the project.

Landscapes

Relax and reminisce about all the beautiful places you've visited—with subtle shading and rich colors, they're a fabulous challenge

Remembrance fields

Stitch this relaxing picture of a lazy, hazy, late-summer poppy field, a perfect piece to work and quietly reflect on

The eleventh hour of the eleventh day of the eleventh month, Veterans Day, is when we remember those who have fallen in battle, and of course, we wear a red poppy, too. In creating this design, Maria has captured a great deal of meaning in quite a simple picture. It draws you in while stitching and then again gazing at your handiwork afterwards. Maria told us, "It's more of a painting in thread than a landscape study. If you can, imagine big splodges of red oil paint rather than watercolor—thick rich color."

- 16ct aida, 17x19in (43x48cm) white (or 32ct evenweave)
- Embroidery floss, as listed in the key
- Frame, with a 8¾x10½in (22x26.5cm) aperture, gold

➤ Preparing your fabric

There are several different close tones of color used in this design to achieve the shading of poppies and greenery. Therefore, it will be crucial to count carefully as you are stitching to ensure you don't stitch the wrong color in the wrong place. To help you with this, stitch horizontal and vertical tacking lines across your fabric, spaced about 20 squares apart. Mark the corresponding lines on your chart; then you can easily see where you are while stitching. Also, as this is a very densely stitched design, your fabric can easily distort. Therefore, it's very important to work with your fabric mounted in either an embroidery hoop or frame.

Stitching the design

All the cross stitch is worked in two strands over one thread of the aida fabric. Make sure you refer carefully to the chart and key to ensure you are using the correct shade of thread as you work. The half cross stitch is worked in two strands. To do this, simply work one diagonal stitch to make a half cross, making sure that all your stitches face in the same direction. This is worked on the furthest light grey-green field on the horizon and all the sky and clouds. Half cross stitch gives your work depth and makes the foreground more dominant. This helps to give the sense of perspective needed for a landscape scene.

Adding the details

When you have finished working all the cross stitch, you can add the backstitch details, which are mostly on the poppies in the foreground. These are worked in one strand: Dark brown for the tree outline and details and Dark grey for the poppies. Do take care while you are working the backstitch round the poppies, as they are quite intricate and will require careful counting. Also, take care not to pull the thread too firmly, as the backstitches have a tendency to disappear between the already worked cross stitches. Finally, work some of the poppy centers as French knots using one strand of dark grey embroidery floss.

Backstitch tip

When you are working backstitch over already worked cross stitches, as with the poppies, it's important to stitch slowly. This is because if you pull the thread too quickly your backstitches can easily get lost between the cross stitches or not lie straight. Hold the thread where you want the backstitch to be, then pull the needle and thread slowly until the backstitch sits just on top of the cross stitches and lies straight.

Remembrance fields

	DMC	Anchor	Madeira	Color
Cross stitch in two strands				
♥▮♥	304	019	0511	Dark red
▫▫▫	352	009	0303	Coral
▨▨	606	334	0209	Bright red
★▮★	642	392	1903	Dark grey green
♡▮♡	817	013	0211	Light red
⌧▮⌧	839	1086	1913	Dark brown
#▮#	840	1084	1912	Light brown
◆▮◆	895	1044	1405	Very dark green
▶◀	936	846	1507	Moss green
▲▮▲	947	330	0205	Dark orange
△▮△	970	925	0204	Light orange
@▮@	3345	268	1406	Dark green
◎▮◎	3346	267	1407	Medium green
⛝▮⛝	3347	266	1408	Light green
·▮·	3348	264	1409	Very light green
★▮★	3778	1013	2312	Light brick
★▮★	3830	5975	0401	Dark brick
Half cross stitch in two strands				
=▮=	334	977	1003	Dark blue
~▮~	415	398	1802	Light grey
2▮2	519	1038	1105	Medium blue
⧄⧄	524	858	1511	Light grey green
+▮+	828	9159	1014	Light blue
Backstitch in one strand				
——	*839	1086	1913	Dark brown
	tree outlines and details			
——	844	1041	1810	Dark grey
	poppy outlines and details			
French knots in one strand				
●●	*844	1041	1810	Dark grey
	poppy centers			

Stitched using DMC threads on 16ct aida
Stitch count 140x167
Design area 8¾x10½in (22x26.5cm)
*indicates color is listed earlier in the key

The sky is worked in half cross stitch to bring out the foreground details, while some of the poppies are highlighted by French knots and a little backstitch

The challenge for this design lies in the close colors that give the plants, trees and sheep their detailed look, using only some backstitch in addition

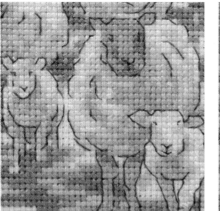 

Spring lambs

The lambs have arrived, leaves unfurl, blossom is erupting and spring flowers burst into color—it's a beautiful spring day

After a long, dark winter it's always a joy to welcome the wonders of the spring and Maria's scene captures so much of what makes this season so good. There's new life in the form of the spring lambs, gamboling along with their mums, while around them all sorts of plants are welcoming the warmer weather with new growth. There are bluebells creating a luscious carpet of color on the ground and blossom in the trees. So, even if you can't get out to the country, the spring comes to you in stitches! ➤

➤ Getting started

The details in this design are not achieved using fractional stitches, but with several close shades of the same color—mainly green. When you have lots of close shades it's worth taking time to identify your skeins with the key and each symbol. Do this in good daylight, as when you are stitching by artificial light, the colors can look quite similar.

Stitching the design

All the cross stitch is worked in two strands of embroidery floss over one thread of the aida fabric. As the design is densely stitched and the colors very similar, you may find it helps with counting to cross off your stitches as you go on the chart. Use fluorescent highlighter pens for this, as you will still be able to see the chart symbol

Spring lambs

Cross stitch in two strands

	DMC	Anchor	Madeira	Color
·⊡·	White	002	2402	White
❸❸	316	1017	0809	Violet
∎∎	319	1044	1313	Very dark green
⊞⊞	320	215	1311	Medium green
△⊿△	340	118	0902	Light purple
≤⊠≤	367	216	1312	Dark green
⊠⊠	368	214	1310	Light green
▢▢	369	1043	1309	Very light green
▷▷	402	1047	2307	Apricot
◆◆	469	267	1503	Dark leaf green
@@	470	266	1502	Medium leaf green
⒉⒉	471	265	1501	Light moss green
∩∩	472	253	1414	Light leaf green
◆◆	640	393	1905	Dark green grey
#⊡#	642	392	1903	Medium green grey
◇◇	644	391	1902	Straw
◀◀	646	8581	1812	Medium grey
⊠⊠	647	1040	1813	Light green grey
⒬⒬	648	397	1814	Light grey
⋆⋆	727	293	0110	Light yellow
★★	742	303	0114	Orange
☆☆	743	302	0113	Dark yellow
~~	746	275	0101	Pale yellow
●●	937	268	1504	Dark moss green
♥♥	962	075	0609	Dark pink
++	3072	900	1805	Pale blue grey
♡♡	3716	025	0606	Light pink
▲▲	3746	119	2702	Dark purple
⋈⋈	3790	904	1905	Brown

Half cross stitch in two strands

⒉⒉	334	977	1003	Dark blue
④④	775	128	1001	Light blue
⊡⊡	3325	129	1002	Sky blue

Backstitch in one strand

—	844	1041	1810	Dark grey
	all other outlines and details			
—	*3790	904	1905	Brown
	fence outlines and details			

Stitched using DMC threads on 16ct aida
Stitch count 112x140
Design area 7x8¾in (18x22.5cm)

*indicates color is listed earlier in the key

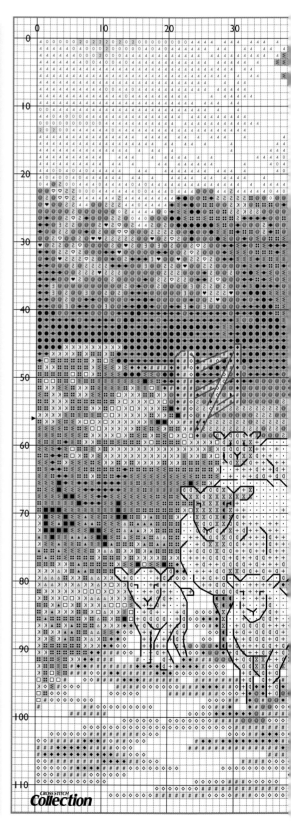

beneath them. These pens can be bought in many colors and different thicknesses.

Working the sky

The sky is worked in half cross stitch using two strands of embroidery floss. Again, the colors are fairly close in shade, so do take care to use the right one. Work all your half crosses in the same direction, preferably the same as that of the top half of the full cross stitches.

Adding the details

When you have finished all the cross stitch you can add the backstitch details. These are worked using one strand: Brown for the fence outlines and details and Dark grey for the other details.

Bare branches are worked in backstitch, standing out against the glowing sunset, while some of the snow is unstitched, but could be stitched in white thread

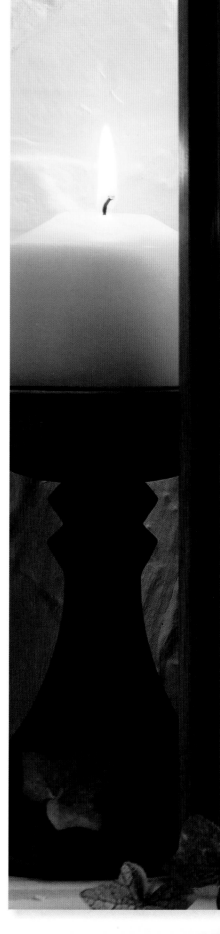

Sunset trail

Take a walk in the woods, with the snow crunching under your feet, and enjoy the beauty of this winter sunset scene

D eer are shy and elusive creatures, usually bounding off into the woods at the slightest disturbance. Maria has captured this stag wandering down a trail and looking back to see us watching beautifully. In another few seconds he will be gone into the woods, leaving us with just the glow of the winter sun in the clouds and sky as it sets below the horizon. It's a perfect moment in time, captured in stitches for you, and maybe it will bring back memories of your own times spent enjoying the beautiful sights that the natural world gives us. ➤

A closer look...

"Once again, I seem to have designed something that I feel evokes a specific mood or moment in time. I can practically feel the warm spring sun as it dances across the new leaves. Those lovely fresh days when an invigorating walk (or in my case, a desperate attempt to wear out the children!) just lifts your spirits."

Before you begin

➤ This is a deceptively easy design to stitch, even though nearly all the fabric is covered in stitching. The subtle shading of the bluebells and the light filtering through the trees is achieved not by fractional stitches, but by many color changes of full cross stitch with a little backstitch. The only thing you really need to watch is your counting. There are lots of different shades of the same color used, so it's important to identify each one on the key and chart before you begin. It will help if you sort them all on to a thread organizer, just to be sure you don't get them mixed up. As you stitch, always double check you are using the correct color and count your stitches, then count again! This will save a lot of unpicking later on.

Working the design

Fold your fabric in half both ways to find the center and begin stitching from this point. All the cross stitch is worked in two strands of embroidery floss over two threads of the evenweave fabric. You could use 14ct aida instead and work over one thread, as there is very little fabric showing, but do make sure you use a similar pale grey color so it blends well with the stitching. When you have finished working all the cross stitch, you can add the backstitch details. These are all worked using one strand of brown embroidery floss.

Making the **frame**

You will need:
- ✦ Frame—untreated wood
- ✦ Wood primer and undercoat
- ✦ Small tester pot of matching emulsion
- ✦ Varnish

This is such a subtle, pretty design, we decided it needed a matching frame. You may be lucky enough to find just the right frame at your local framers, but if you don't, then it's relatively simple to customize your own.

1. Ask your framer to make a plain, untreated wooden frame to fit your finished design.
2. Paint the frame with a couple of coats of combined wood primer and undercoat.
3. Now take your stitched design to the paint shop and choose a paint sample in a color to coordinate with the design. We chose a shade in the mid range of the bluebells.

Paint two or three coats of this on to your frame until you get a good even coverage.

4. When the paint is really dry, seal it with two coats of varnish. There are speciality varnishes you can buy that are designed for painting on top of emulsion, particularly for wall murals. Ask at your local decorating shop for advice. They can be bought in matt, satin or gloss finish depending on which effect you want to create.
5. Mount your stitching into the finished frame in the usual way.

Bluebell wood

DMC	Anchor	Madeira	Color
Cross stitch in two strands			
155	109	0803	Dark amethyst
161	122	0905	Very dark bluebell
340	118	0902	Light amethyst
341	117	2711	Light bluebell
368	214	1310	Dark peppermint
371	885	2111	Olive
414	235	1801	Grey
469	267	1503	Dark leaf green
470	266	1502	Medium leaf green
472	253	1414	Light leaf green
522	860	1513	Dark grey green
523	859	1510	Light grey green
580	924	1608	Moss
611	898	2107	Khaki
642	392	1813	Light graphite
644	391	1814	Dark cream
646	1040	1811	Pewter
704	255	1308	Light bright green
772	259	1604	Light peppermint
793	176	0906	Dark bluebell
794	175	0907	Medium bluebell
822	390	1908	Light cream
906	256	1411	Dark bright green
926	850	1707	Light petrol blue
3022	8581	1812	Dark graphite
3078	292	0102	Yellow
3348	264	1409	Light green
3363	262	1602	Dark green
3364	261	1603	Medium green
3747	120	0901	Very light bluebell
3756	1037	2504	Pale blue
3768	779	2508	Dark petrol blue
3838	940	2702	Lavender
3847	1076	2507	Turquoise

	DMC	Anchor	Madeira	Color
Backstitch in one strand				
—	3790	903	1905	Brown
	all outlines and details			

Stitched using DMC threads on 28ct evenweave over two threads

Stitch count 140x112 Design area 10x8in (25x20cm)

Wisteria cottage

You can't help but be transported by this beautiful cottage scene and picture yourself relaxing on the lawn as you admire the flowering wisteria

Florals

Celebrate new beginnings with the blossoms of spring—from traditional designs inspired by great artists, to modern interpretations

Sumptuous pinks and the regal gold backstitch, which offers a great alternative to the usual black, give this design a truly luxurious feel

 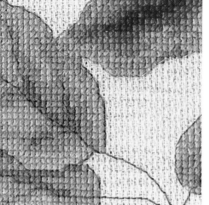

Floral
vintage

The classic peony is given a fantastic modern makeover with bold colors and an ultra-stylish frameless finish

An eye-popping floral wall decoration is a must-have for any stylish home, and when you can stitch something as professional-looking as this gorgeous peony, who needs to go looking for an art print? The design's vintage pinks and greens are right on trend at the moment, and it is stitched on a lovely textured rustic aida to give it that classic look.

Mounting the finished design as a stretched canvas draws all the focus on to the peony itself without the distraction of a frame. ➤

Shopping list...

- 14ct linen aida, natural, 15¾x15¾in (40x40cm) (or 28ct linen)
- Embroidery floss, as listed in the key
- Frame with a 9x9in (23x23cm) outer dimension
- Felt, white, 9x9in (23x23cm), for backing
- Tapestry needle, size 24

➤ Stitching the design

Fold your fabric in half both ways to find the center and start stitching at this point. All the cross stitch is worked in three strands of embroidery floss over one thread of the aida fabric.

Adding the details

When you have finished all the cross stitch, you can add the backstitch details. These are worked using one embroidery floss and one strand of DMC Light Effects metallic thread.

Framing your picture

Ask your framer for a flat, plain wooden frame about 1in (2.5cm) deep cut to the dimensions given in the shopping list. The sizes stated are the outer dimensions of the frame. This isn't how we would normally give a frame size, but for this sort of stretched canvas effect, the outside size is the most important one. Also, ask the framer to cut a piece of white mount board to fit exactly over the finished frame.

1. Stick the mount board on top of the frame with double-sided tape.
2. Place your finished stitching centrally over that and push pins through the edge of the fabric and into the mount board.
3. Stick double-sided tape over the back of the frame and stretch the fabric tightly round to the back and stick into place. Fold the corners neatly so you have a 90° angle at the edges.
4. Stitch the piece of felt over the back of the frame for a neater effect.

Metallic backstitch tip

When working your metallic backstitch, be sure to only stitch across one aida block at a time. This will ensure your thread lies flat against the fabric and doesn't split or come loose. Use short lengths of this as it can fray when being constantly pulled through the fabric.

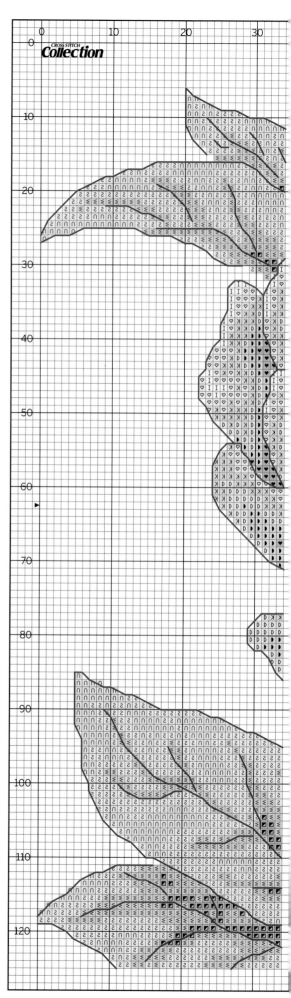

Floral vintage

DMC	Anchor	Madeira	Color
Cross stitch in three strands			
×× White	002	2402	White
♡♡ 352	009	0303	Light red
II 353	008	2605	Very light red
JJ 727	293	0110	Light yellow
◨◨ 732	281	1612	D olive green
≋≋ 733	280	1611	M olive green
⊇⊇ 734	279	1610	L olive green
◊◊ 743	302	0113	Dark yellow
~~ 754	1012	0305	Pink beige
⋈⋈ 777	043	0513	Very dark red
nn 3046	887	2206	Sand
×× 3712	1023	0406	Light red
♥♥ 3831	1006	0507	Dark pink
▶▶ 3832	028	0506	Medium red
DD 3833	1023	0609	Pink
XX 3853	1003	0311	Dark orange
33 3854	313	2301	Light orange

DMC	Anchor	Madeira	Color
Backstitch in one strand			
— 730	845	1614	V d olive green
leaves, stem			
— *3853	1003	0311	Dark orange
flower centers			
— DMC Light Effects E3852			
peony			

Stitched using DMC threads on 14ct aida
Stitch count 125x126
Design area 9x9in (23x23cm)

*indicates color is listed earlier in the key

A rich and vivid color palette makes this design stand out—it's the perfect addition to a modern or traditional home

Floral fancy

Maria's tulip makes a stunning focal point for your home. It will brighten up any room and inject spring vivacity all year round

This shocking pink tulip is perfectly formed and ready to cheer up any tired décor. With its rich raspberry shades and realistic look, it will be a treat to stitch as well as look spectacular when it's finished and mounted on the wall. Despite its size, only whole stitches are used, so there's nothing too tricky involved in the project, just remember to separate your threads beforehand. We opted for a stretch canvas finish to make the most of the tulip's stylish angle. ➤

➤ Stitching the design

All the cross stitch is worked in three strands of embroidery floss over one thread of the aida fabric. As the design is densely stitched and the colors very similar, you may find it helps with counting to cross off your stitches as you go on the chart. Use fluorescent highlighter pens for this, as you will still be able to see the chart symbol beneath them after you have crossed them out.

It's easy for fabric to become puckered and distorted, especially when a design is heavily stitched like this one. To help prevent this from happening, invest in a roller frame to keep your fabric as taut as possible. Not only will you find it easier to work the design, but it will also help to create even stitching.

Color change tip

For an immediate change that will give your design a totally different look, stitch your tulip on to a pale pink aida instead.

Organizing your threads

Every stitcher has a different way of organizing their threads, but it really would help when stitching this design to make a thread organizer. You can make your own by punching holes in a piece of thin card then writing the color number and symbol by each hole and looping the relevant thread through it. Alternatively, wind each skein on to a card bobbin and label these in the same way. This does take time initially, but it will save time in the long-run by not getting confused with similar shades while you are stitching.

Adding the details

When you have finished all the cross stitch you can add the backstitch details. These are all worked using one strand of embroidery floss.

Refer to page 68 for framing your stitching.

Floral fancy

DMC	Anchor	Madeira	Color
Cross stitch in three strands			
150	042	0703	Dark red
164	240	1209	Leaf green
353	008	2605	Apricot
561	212	1205	Dark green
562	210	1206	Medium green
563	208	1207	Light green
600	059	0704	Very dark pink
602	057	0702	Dark pink
603	062	0701	Medium pink
777	043	0514	Ruby
3078	292	0102	Yellow
3350	077	0603	Light red
3716	025	0606	Light pink
3770	1009	2314	Pink beige

DMC	Anchor	Madeira	Color
Backstitch in one strand			
━ 902	897	0601	Wine
all outlines and details			

Stitched using DMC threads on 14ct aida
Stitch count 117x118
Design area 8¼x8½in (21x21cm)

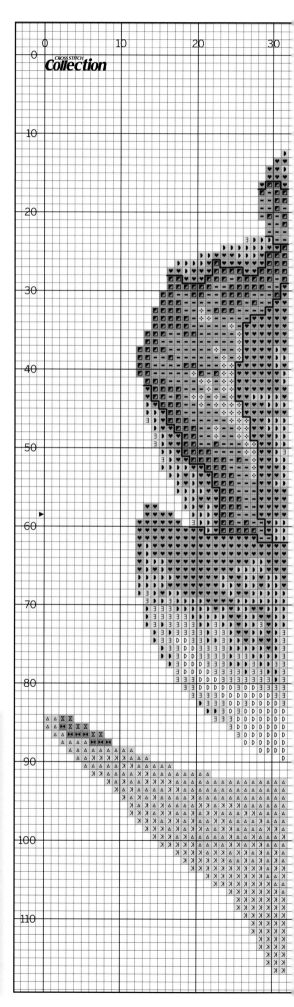

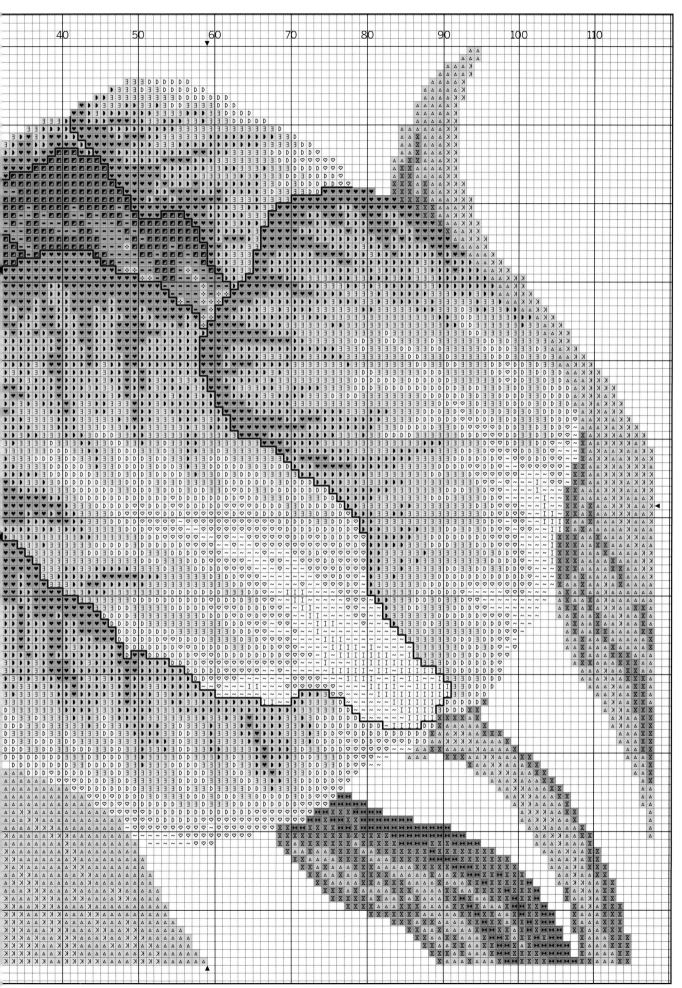

Colors bloom **when you stitch with three strands, and the backstitches provide lifelike texture on the stem and bud**

 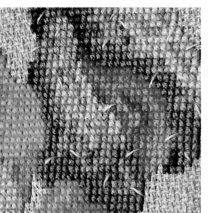

Scarlet statement

Bring an explosion of color into your home with this dazzling poppy project. The flower's vibrant reds and oranges will brighten any room

This is your chance to be inspired by the beauty of nature and create a really dramatic, eye-catching decoration to hang on your wall. We're bowled over by the striking colors, and to emphasize the rich reds, we decided to stretch our finished poppy over a canvas instead of framing it. Clusters of deep purple seed beads really bring the design to life, catching the light and giving it a natural feel. Try using a thread organizer to help distinguish between the stunning array of red and orange shades. ➤

Shopping list...

♦ 14ct linen aida, natural, 11¾x11¾in (30x30cm) (or 28ct linen)
♦ Embroidery floss, as listed in the key
♦ Frame, with a 8½x8½in (22x22cm) outer dimension,
♦ Beads, as listed in the key

Stitching the design

Fold your fabric in half both ways to find the center and start stitching from this point. All the cross stitch is worked in three strands of embroidery floss over one thread of the aida fabric. This design is stitched using three strands of cotton for better coverage on the aida so that the fabric does not show through. Stitching in three strands also makes the most of the rich color palette.

There are several colors that are fairly similar in shade used in this design. For this reason, do take care to select the correct one each time as you are working. This is particularly important when working in artificial light.

Adding the details

When you have finished all the cross stitch, you can add the backstitch details. These are worked using one strand of embroidery floss: Magenta for the petals and Light green for the other details.

Attaching the beads

The beads are attached to the fabric when all the other stitching is finished. Both bugle beads and seed beads are used in this design. Use a thread that matches the fabric or the cross stitches underneath. Work a half cross stitch through the bead, making sure that the bead doesn't sag on the fabric by working a couple of tiny backstitches behind it to hold it tight.

Ironing your work tip

It will be much easier to press your design before adding the beads. Alternatively, cushion the beads by placing your stitching on a fluffy towel to prevent them from being crushed as you iron the poppy. Always remember to iron delicate projects like this on a low heat setting.

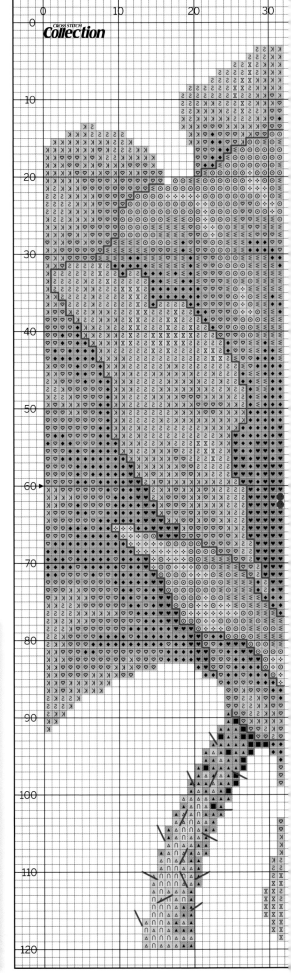

Scarlet statement

	DMC	Anchor	Madeira	Color
Cross stitch in three strands				
▶◀	154	070	1810	Dark purple
♥♥	498	1005	0511	Dark red
■■	500	683	1705	V dark green
✦✦	603	052	0701	Baby pink
♡♡	606	335	0209	Bright red
⊠⊠	608	332	0206	Bright orange
◆◆	666	046	0210	Medium red
⊠⊠	741	304	0201	Light orange
◎◎	892	028	0412	Dark pink
⌇⌇	970	316	0204	Dark orange
▲▲	987	244	1403	Dark green
◢◣	989	241	1401	Med green
∩∩	3348	264	1409	Leaf green
I I	3706	033	0409	Light pink
▶▶	3740	873	2614	Plum
≤≤	3801	1098	0411	Light red
D D	3834	100	0805	Med purple
⊡⊡	3835	098	0712	Light purple

	DMC	Anchor	Madeira	Color
Backstitch in one strand				
——	369	1043	1309	Light green
all other outlines and details				
——	718	089	0707	Magenta
petals				

Attach beads with matching cotton

●●	seed beads	Rainbow
flower center		
●●	seed beads	Black
flower center		
▬	bugle bead	Royal mauve
flower center		

Stitched using DMC threads on 14ct aida
Stitch count 120x120
Design area 8½x8½in (22x22cm)

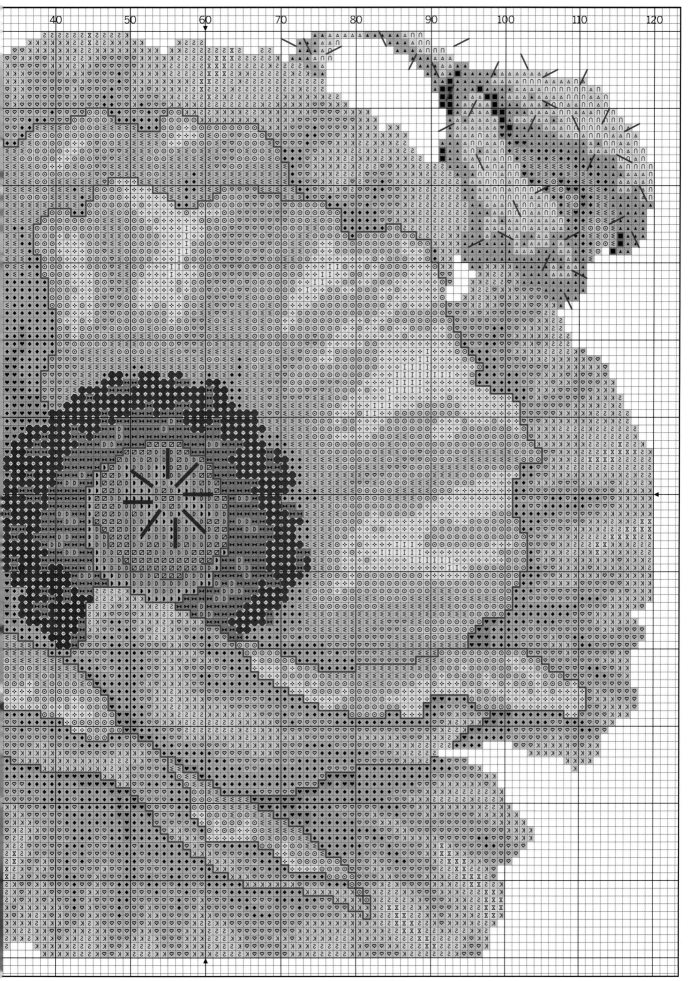

Fresh as a daisy

Stitch yourself some super accessories by making this sweet and simple daisy set, consisting of a needle case, scissor keep and pin cushion

Busy stitchers can rapidly wear out their accessories, and it's always nice to be able to stitch up your own new handy items once in a while, so this fresh and bright daisy sewing set is ideal. Maria had a great time designing them, "I like doing more modern, fun things, so here I have stitched the daisies as if they were pressed flowers. With the excluded line creating a sort of negative border, which is greatly enhanced by the gold thread on the colored fabric."

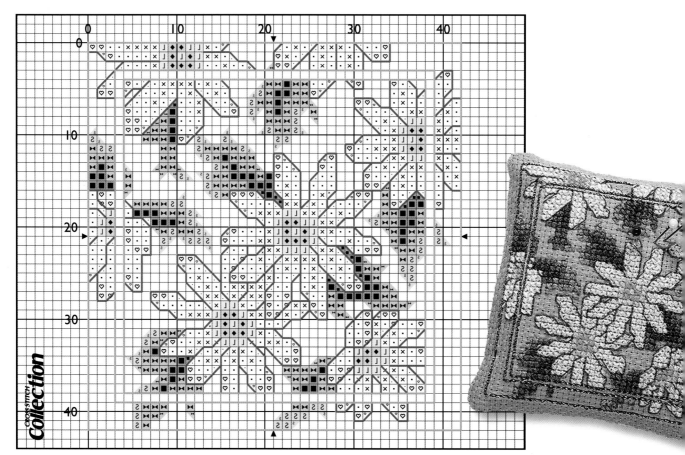

➤ Starting stitching

This lovely daisy sewing set has a really cheerful design. The background of pale blue aida really gives the design depth and highlights the daisies. There are quite a few fractional stitches to shape the petals and leaves, but if you work one daisy at a time, they will be easier to place.

Start in the center of your fabric and work outwards. There is a very subtle color change between the pale blue and white thread. Working in good light will help to identify such areas in the daisies. Stitch the border last so that the backstitch sits neatly over the design. When stitching with metallic threads, it is a good idea to use a tapestry needle, as this will be easier to thread. If you let your thread hang freely as you are working the backstitch, it will unwind naturally and become less likely to twist. This will make the stitches neat and smooth.

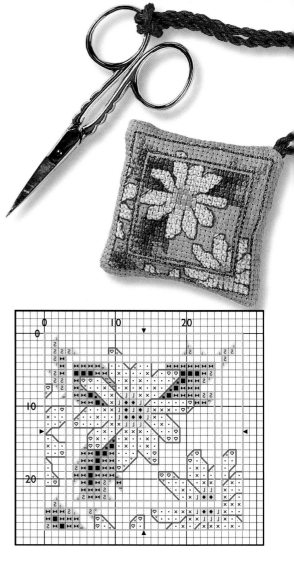

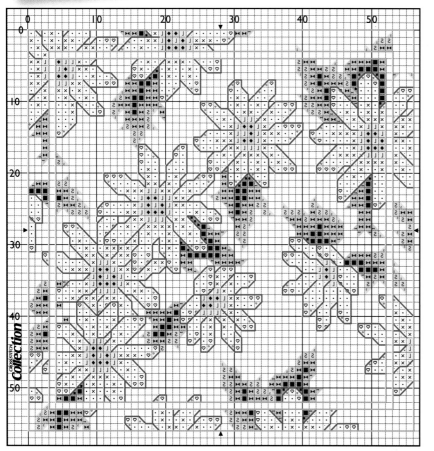

Fresh as a daisy

Cross stitch in three strands

	DMC	Anchor	Madeira	Color
· White	White	002	2402	White
2 2	164	240	1604	Light green
◆◆	741	304	0203	Orange
⌐ ⌐	743	302	0113	Yellow
♡♡	819	271	0501	Pink
■■	987	244	1403	Dark green
⋈⋈	989	242	1401	Medium green
✕✕	3756	1037	2504	Pale blue

Backstitch in two strands

——— DMC Light Effects E3852
    borders

Backstitch in one strand

———	798	146	0911	Blue

daisies

Stitched using DMC threads on 14ct aida
Needle case stitch count 56×56
Design area 4×4in (10×10cm)
Pin cushion stitch count 42×42 Design area 3×3in (8×8cm)
Scissor keep stitch count 27×28 Design area 2×2in (5×5cm)

Treasured
words

Keen book readers can indulge in both of their favorite leisure activities by stitching up this beautiful purple iris reading set

Maria was inspired by glass: "I've a passion for the Art Nouveau and Arts and Crafts movements—celebrating the beauty of nature. With Tiffany glass, it has a painterly, watercolor quality, which I've tried to portray in the shading."

Stitching the designs
To start, work the cross stitch in two strands of cotton over one aida block. These designs include fractionals to add shape. You can switch to a sharper embroidery needle to work fractionals. Add the backstitch with one strand of cotton.

Making your bookmark
Using a bright color of thread, tack a line two squares away from the stitching along both sides and also across the top edge of the bookmark. Tack a line at the base at 45 degrees so the point is in the middle. Trim the fabric ½in (1.5cm) ➤

Shopping list...
✦ **14ct aida,** white (or 28ct evenweave). Bookmark: 10x5in (26x13cm). Coaster: 7x7in (18x18cm). Diary: 7x7in (18x18cm)
✦ **Embroidery floss,** as listed in the key
✦ **Felt,** 7¼x2¼in (18.5x6cm) white
✦ **Iron-on interfacing,** 4x4in (10x10cm)
✦ **Embroidery floss,** for the tassel

Treasured words

Cross stitch in two strands

	Anchor	DMC	Madeira	Color
♡♡	108	210	0802	Light purple
♥♥	109	209	0803	Medium purple
◆◆	110	208	0804	Dark purple
~~	128	775	0908	Dark blue
⋈⋈	209	912	1213	Dark green
■■	210	562	1206	Very dark green
2 2	214	368	2604	Medium green
1 1	259	772	1604	Very light green
++	260	3348	1409	Light green
✕✕	342	211	0801	Very light purple
⌡⌡	928	598	1111	Turquoise
·|·	1037	3756	2504	Light blue

Backstitch in one strand

▬	401	413	1713	Grey

all outlines and details

Stitched using Anchor threads on 14ct aida
Diary stitch count 45x45
Design area 3¼x3¼in (8x8cm)

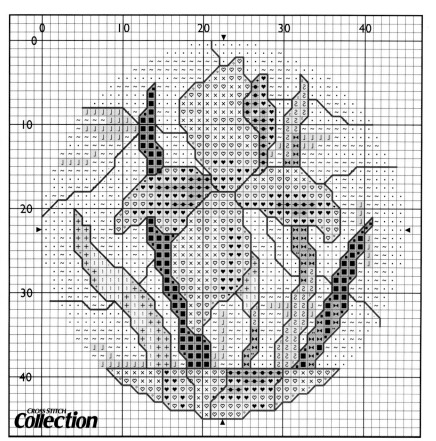

CROSS STITCH
Collection

from the tacked line. Turn under all edges to the wrong side along the tacked lines. Fold the fabric at the corners and pin or tack the hems in place. Make a tassel out of the purple shades of embroidery floss and attach it to the back of the stitching. Trim your felt to the finished shape of the bookmark and place over the back of the stitching. Sew through the felt and hems with small neat stitches, ensuring all raw edges are contained and that the tassel is securely attached. Finally, remove the tacking stitches to complete your bookmark.

Finish a coaster

Trim the finished coaster design to six aida squares from the stitching on all four sides. Fray three rows carefully, then press the iron-on interfacing on to the wrong side.

Make a diary patch

To get the stitching in the middle of the patch for

the diary, first cut a circle in a piece of paper 3½in (9cm) in diameter as a template. Place the template centrally over the stitching and lightly draw around the circle with a pencil. Cut carefully around the pencil line and stick the finished patch on to the front of your diary or journal with double-sided tape.

Treasured words

	Anchor	DMC	Madeira	Color
Cross stitch in two strands				
♡♡♡	108	210	0802	Light purple
♥♥♥	109	209	0803	Medium purple
◆◆◆	110	208	0804	Dark purple
∼∼∼	128	775	0908	Dark blue
⋈⋈⋈	209	912	1213	Dark green
■■■	210	562	1206	Very dark green
2 2 2	214	368	2604	Medium green
1 1 1	259	772	1604	Very light green
+++	260	3348	1409	Light green
×××	342	211	0801	Very light purple
⌐⌐⌐	928	598	1111	Turquoise
·I·	1037	3756	2504	Light blue

Backstitch in one strand

——	401	413	1713	Grey
	all outlines and details			

Stitched using Anchor threads on 14ct aida
Bookmark stitch count 84×28 Design area 6×2in (15×5cm)
Coaster stitch count 56×56 Design area 4×4in (10×10cm)

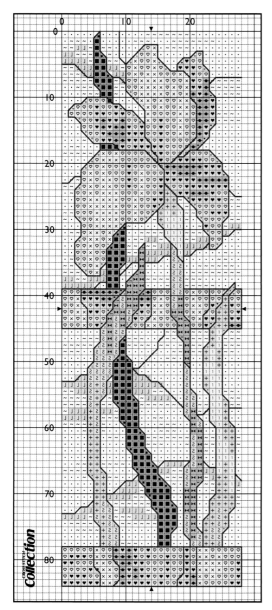

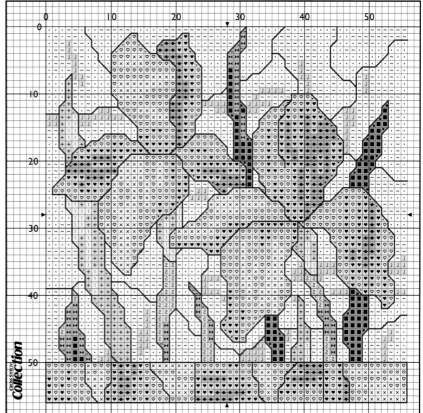

Natural linen makes the perfect background for this **William Morris inspired** design and lets the bright tones of the leaves and flowers show up to their best effect

Art & craft

The work of William Morris in the nineteenth century is still inspiring today, and these bag and purse designs are great examples

The Arts & Crafts movement, inspired by William Morris, has seen a major revival in recent years and it's not hard to see why with the quality of designs like Maria's. William Morris championed decorative arts like embroidery, but his talents extended to the written word as well as design. His legacy is that even now, more than a century after his death, we still find such beauty in his observations of the natural world and we show it through our needlework. ➤

S

Be
ar
pe

- ✦ **14ct aida**, cream, 8x8in (20x20cm) per card (or 28ct evenweave)
- ✦ **Embroidery floss**, as listed in the key
- ✦ **Cards**, square aperture, cream

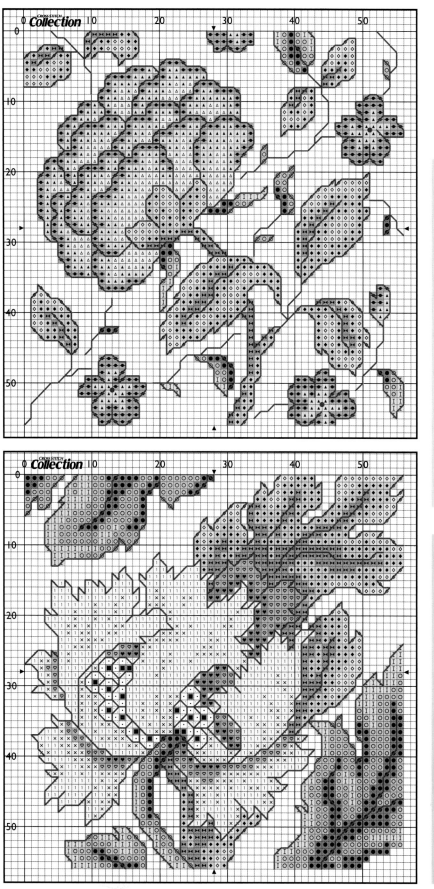

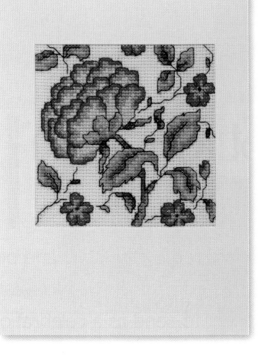

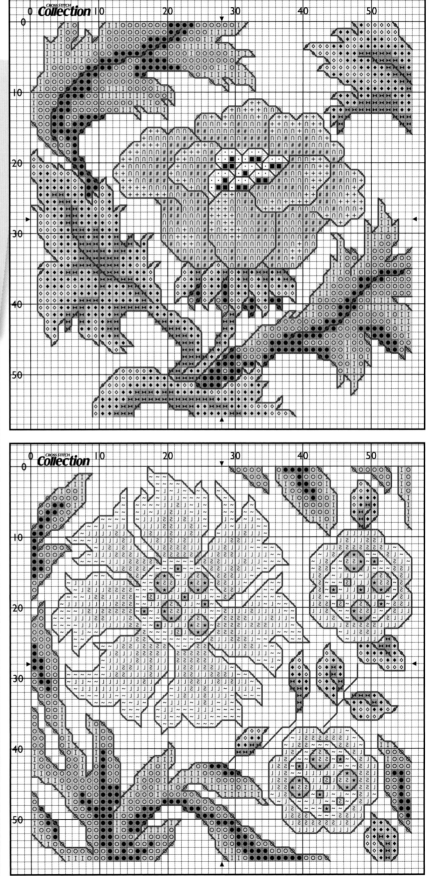

Stitching in harmony

	DMC	Anchor	Madeira	Color
·ı·	White	002	2402	White
▲▲	151	073	0607	Light pink
♥♥	304	019	0511	Dark red
♡♡	349	013	0212	Light red
✕✕	353	008	2605	Coral
◆◆	471	265	1501	Medium green
◇◇	472	253	1414	Light green
●●	561	212	1205	Dark blue green
ЈЈ	726	295	0109	Medium yellow
∩∩	728	306	0113	Light gold
##	783	307	2212	Dark gold
ıı	948	1011	0306	Flesh
𝟤𝟤	972	298	0107	Dark yellow
■■	3031	905	2003	Brown
~~	3078	292	0102	Light yellow
⋈⋈	3346	267	1407	Dark green
◆◆	3350	077	0603	Dark pink
▲▲	3733	075	0504	Medium pink
◯◯	3816	876	1703	Medium blue green
ııı	3817	875	1702	Light blue green
★★	3853	1003	0307	Orange
++	3855	311	2513	Apricot

Backstitch in one strand
—— *3031 905 2003 Brown
all outlines and details

French knots in one strand
●● *3031 905 2003 Brown
small pink flower centers

Stitched using DMC threads on 14ct aida
Stitch count 56x56 Design area 4x4in (10x10cm)
*indicates color is listed earlier in the key

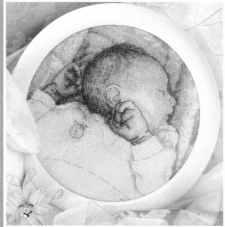

Baby

Sepia tones create a peaceful and soothing mood, perfect for capturing those first special moments shared between newborn and mother

Little angel

Celebrate the most amazing moment in any parent's life with this unique and serenely captivating set of baby designs

Maria has stolen all our hearts lots of times before with her stunning baby pictures, and this set of designs is one of her best! Based on her own childrens' photographs and many fond memories, Maria has captured those special moments and quiet thoughts that every parent can identify with, which you can now recreate in stitches and keep forever.

➤

Sepia shades are all that is used to create the mother and sleeping baby, so great care is needed in making sure the right thread is used for every stitch

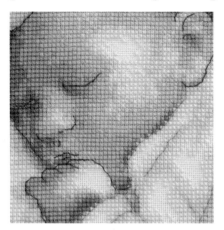

Shopping list...

+ 28ct evenweave, white, main picture, 18×16in (46×41cm) (or 14ct aida)
+ 14ct aida, white, angel photo 14×14in (36×36cm), journal 14×12in (36×31cm) (or 28ct evenweave)
+ Embroidery floss, as listed in the key
+ DMC Light Effects thread, as listed in the key

Main picture
+ Frame, with a 11¼×9¾in (29×25cm) aperture, gilt

Angel photo
+ Frame, with a 6×6in (15×15cm) aperture, blue
+ Interfacing, lightweight iron-on, 8×8in (20×20cm)

Journal
+ Fabric, 7½×5in (19×13cm), beige and blue stripe
+ Notebook, spiral-bound hardback notebook

➤ Starting off

Whichever of the three designs you are stitching, you should start in the center of the fabric. Fold it in half both ways to find this point and mark it with a pin. If you are stitching the 'Angel in the Making' photo design, the area you need to cut out to insert your ultrasound scan photo is marked with a line, so leave this area unstitched.

Stitching the designs

All the cross stitch is worked in two strands of either embroidery floss or DMC Light Effects thread. Refer to the key to see where to place each of the colors. The larger picture is worked on evenweave and each cross stitch is worked over two threads of the fabric. If you are working the photo frame or the journal cover, then work each cross stitch over one thread on aida. You can, of course, work any of the designs on aida or evenweave, as the finished design size will be the same—just choose whichever fabric you prefer to work on.

Adding the details

When you have finished working all the cross stitch, you can add the backstitch details. These are all worked in one strand of embroidery floss, or DMC Light Effects thread and over two threads of the evenweave fabric, or one thread of the aida. There are six different colors of backstitch used in the design, so refer to the key to see which one to use where. The backstitch lines are shown on the chart by different colored lines.

➤

Little angel

DMC	Anchor	Madeira	Color
Cross stitch in two strands			
◇◇ 407	1008	2601	Light sepia
□□ 437	362	2012	Tan
## 632	936	2007	Dark sepia
○○ 712	926	2101	Light cream
⊠⊠ 738	885	2013	Dark cream
∩∩ 739	366	2014	Medium cream
②② 775	128	1001	Blue
◄►◄► 779	360	2005	Very dark sepia
♡♡ 819	271	0501	Pink
♥♥ 3064	882	2312	Dusty pink
△△ 3756	1037	2504	Pale blue
@@ 3772	1007	2311	Medium sepia
③③ DMC Light Effects E3821			

Backstitch in one strand

	DMC	Anchor	Madeira	Color
—	*632	936	2007	Dark sepia
	alphabet and numbers, baby feet and 'angel in the making' frame outlines and details			
—	642	392	2112	Olive
	wings and clothing outlines and details			
—	*779	360	2005	Very dark sepia
	hand and baby face details			
—	3781	905	2003	Brown
	head and face outlines			
—	3864	376	1910	Very light sepia
	lettering and oval outline			
—	*DMC Light Effects E3821			
	star outline			

Stitching guide

— Use as a guide for cutting an aperture for the small 'Angel in the making' photo frame

Stitched using DMC threads on 28ct evenweave over two threads
Picture stitch count 133×105
Design area 9½×7½in (24×19cm)
Stitched using DMC threads on 14ct aida
Photo frame stitch count 75×74
Design area 5¼×5¼in (14×13cm)
Journal stitch count 79×48
Design area 5¾×3½in (14×9cm)

*indicates color is listed earlier in the key

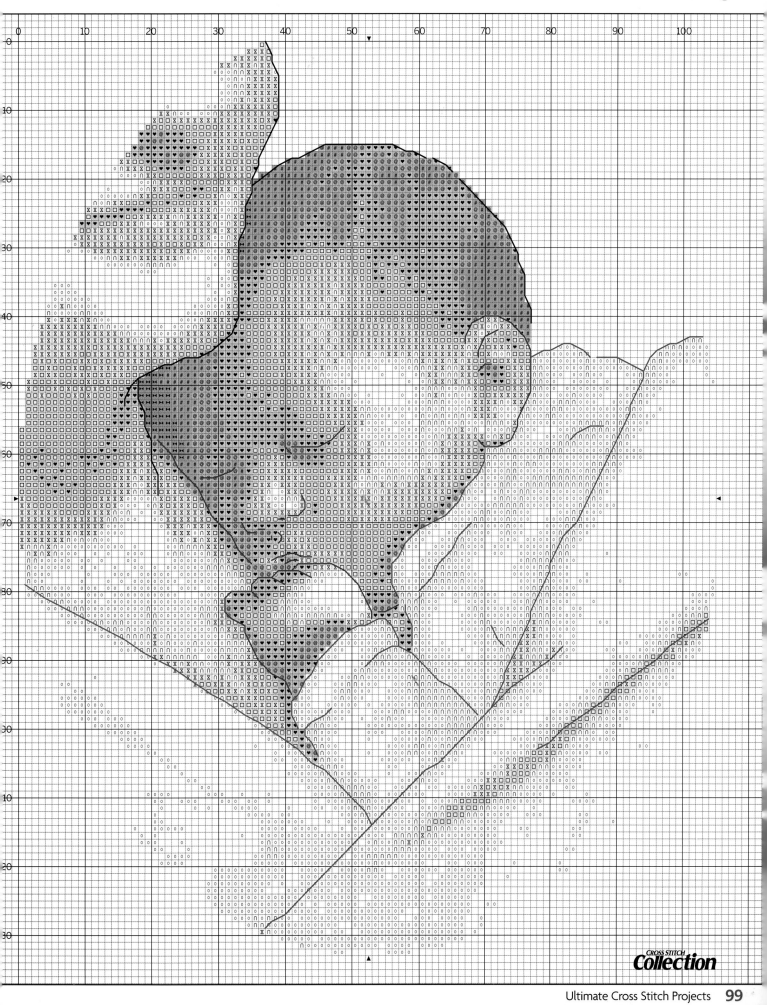

Extras for you...

Stitch this sweet extra project to hold a treasured ultrasound picture…

Framing the angel photo

1. When you have finished all the stitching, wash and press your fabric in the usual way, making sure it is completely dry before continuing.
2. Place the interfacing centrally over the wrong side of the stitching and press firmly into place. This is stuck to the fabric to prevent the aperture for the photograph from fraying.
3. Now, following the lines marked out on the chart, cut out the photograph aperture using sharp scissors.

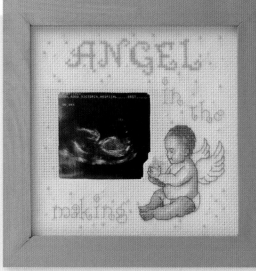

4. Position your ultrasound scan centrally behind the aperture and hold in place using small pieces of adhesive tape.
5. You can now frame the project in the usual way.

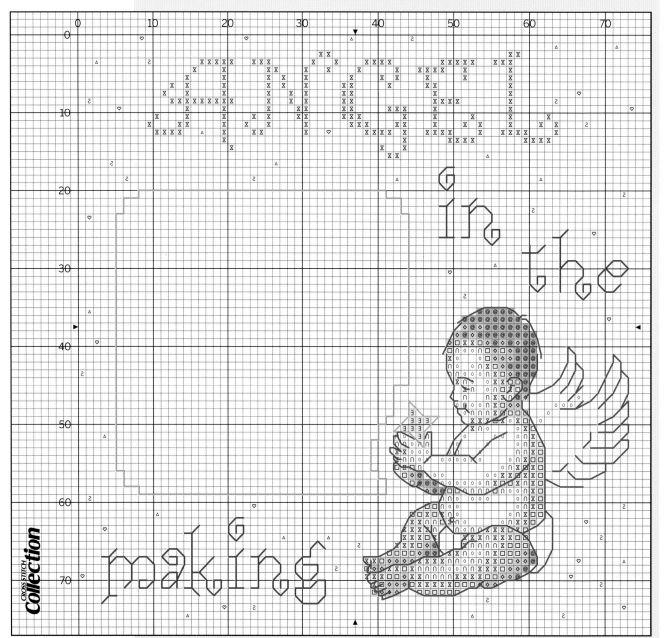

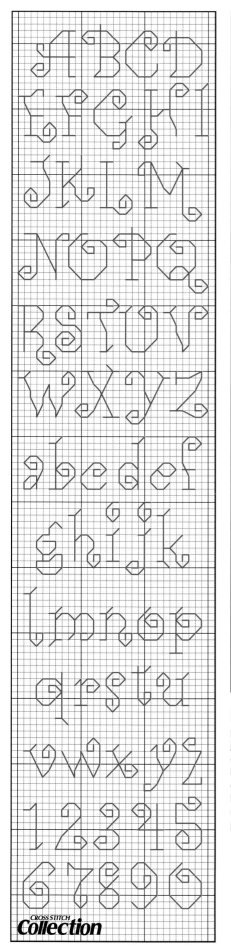

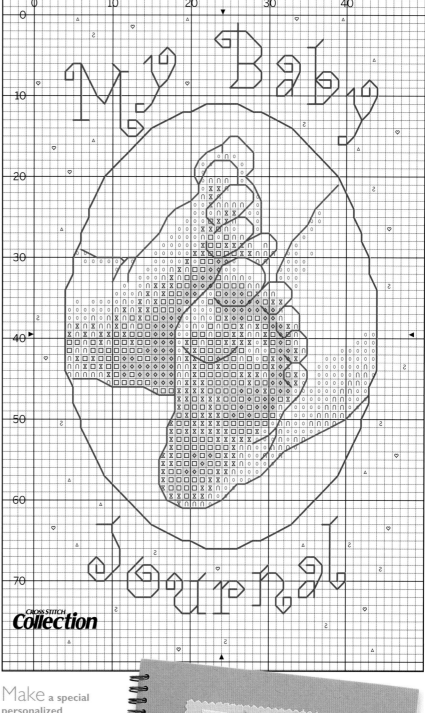

Make a special
personalized
journal to chart all
of your baby's firsts
by attaching your
design to a ring
bound hardback
notebook—it's the
perfect keepsake!

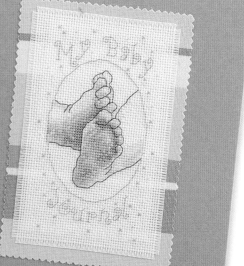

Classic touches make this pretty design so enchanting, like the scattered flowers on the wallpaper and the children's toys on the shelves

Tales from the
toy room

This special rocking horse sampler is well-suited for any nursery or child's bedroom—and it'll become a gift to treasure in the family for a lifetime, too

Maria has put so much thought and detail into this design, from the horse's flowing mane, to the little toys on the shelf and the rose wallpaper—it's the perfect addition to any child's room. The rocking horse is brought to life by different shades of brown, so to save time, why not thread up several needles before you begin and then 'stitch and park'? Maria has even included an alphabet so that your child's name can be added along the bottom of the rocking horse to personalize the piece. ➤

➤ Stitching the design

All the cross stitch is worked in two strands of embroidery floss over one thread of the aida fabric. This design requires careful counting. However, if you divide it into sections it will feel more achievable as you are working. You will find it easier if you work one section at a time rather than trying to work all the stitches of the same color. Keep checking your stitching against the chart as you go, particularly when working the flower stems, as it important for the placement of the other parts that you work these correctly.

Adding the details

When you have finished all the cross stitch, you can add the backstitch details. These are worked using one strand of embroidery floss. There are four different colors of backstitch used and they are each represented with a different colored line on the chart. Use Dark green for the flower stems; Grey for the clock, shelves and wood panelling; Medium red for the lettering, reins, stirrups, kite string and pencils; and Dark sepia for all the other outlines and details.

   Try to avoid trailing your threads across the back of your fabric. Dark or brightly colored threads will create unsightly shadows on the front of your design in areas that have been left unstitched. So always finish your thread off before moving on to the next area.

Tales from the toy room

Cross stitch in two strands

	DMC	Anchor	Madeira	Color
×××	White	002	2402	White
▲▲▲	164	240	1401	Dark green
♡♡♡	351	010	0214	Medium red
+++	353	008	2605	Light red
▲▲▲	369	1043	1309	Light green
◆◆◆	435	365	2010	Dark brown
◇◇◇	437	362	2012	Light brown
⌐⌐⌐	712	926	2101	Light cream
222	739	366	2014	Dark cream
~~	745	300	0111	Yellow
111	746	275	0101	Magnolia
···	762	234	1804	Pale grey
♥♥♥	817	013	0211	Dark red
⁄⁄⁄	822	390	1908	Stone
■■■	839	1086	1913	Dark sepia
⍺⍺⍺	3755	140	1013	Dark blue
★⋅★	3756	1037	2504	Pale blue
III	3841	1032	0908	Light blue
●●●	3863	1084	1911	Medium sepia
⊙⊙⊙	3864	1082	1910	Light sepia

Backstitch in one strand

	DMC	Anchor	Madeira	Color
——	*164	240	1401	Dark green
	flower stems			
——	318	235	1802	Grey
	clock, shelves, wood panelling			
——	*351	010	0214	Medium red
	lettering, reins, stirrups, kite string, pencils			
——	*839	1086	1913	Dark sepia
	all other outlines and details			

Stitched using DMC threads on 14ct aida
Stitch count 83×82
Design area 5¾×5¾in (15×15cm)
*indicates color is listed earlier in the key

Personalize...
your design

To personalize your design, we have provided you with an alphabet. Draw out and plan the name you want to stitch on the empty grid provided. If you need extra space, you could leave out the floral motifs.

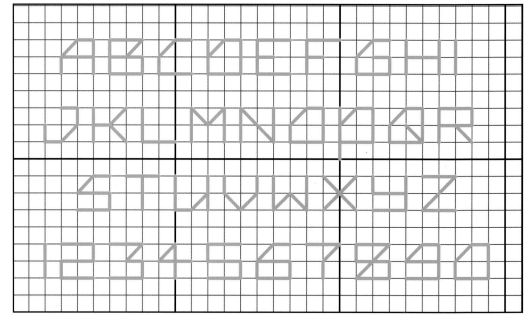

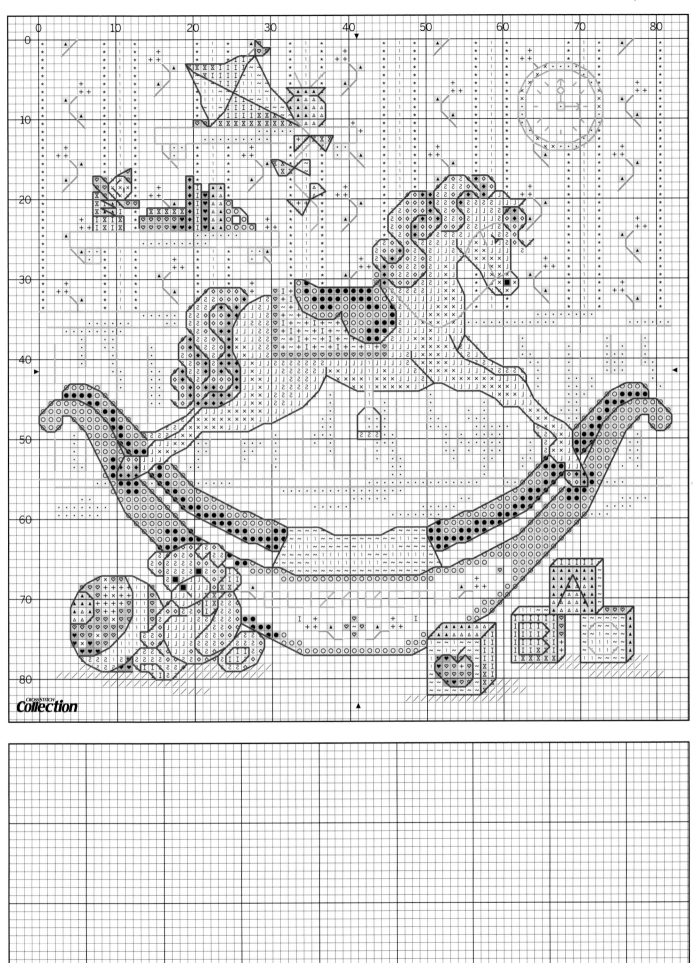

It's amazing what can be conveyed in cross stitch with just a few stitches, subtle color changes and a little backstitch, which combine to create a portrait with such feeling

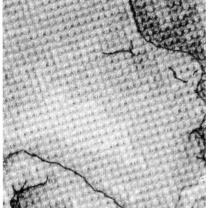

Precious gift

Maria's newborn baby designs are so well loved because of their soft shades and perfectly captivating portraiture

Maria's baby portrait piece of her son Hudson is the ideal gift to any mother. This beautiful design is fairly simple to stitch, in that there are no fractional stitches, and the whole design is worked in whole cross stitch with just a little backstitch. It is worked on a white evenweave so the background area is less prominent against the cross stitches. However, it is worked in ten different shades of sepia embroidery floss, so you will have to make sure you work very carefully to achieve the correct tonal effect.

➤

Extras for you...

Get more from your stitching with these extra projects…

These easy-to-make extras make lovely gifts for a new arrival.

Making the **frame mount**

1. Using double-sided tape, stick the batting over the pre-cut mount, trim the edges to fit and cut out the rectangle in the center. Make it ¼in (6mm) smaller so the batting protrudes over the edge of the cut out aperture.

2. Place the gingham fabric right-side down, then put the batted mount centrally on top of it. Stick double-sided tape all the way around the edge of the back of the mount and round the edge of the central aperture. Stretch the fabric tightly over to the back and stick it onto the tape.

3. Cut out the center of fabric but make the aperture 1in (2½cm) smaller all the way round than the card aperture. Snip diagonally into each corner, then fold the edge of the fabric over to the wrong side of the mount. Stick some masking tape over the top of the folded edges to make it secure.

4. Put the fabric mount inside the frame with the stretched and batted cross stitch behind it.

Name size tip
If you decide to stitch a name using the alphabet, you'll find it much easier to calculate the size and get the spacing correct if you draw out the name onto a piece of graph paper before you start.

Making the **initial patch**

1. Stitch an initial, then cut it out ½in (1½cm) outside the edge of the stitching all the way round.

2. Bind one edge of the patch at a time by placing the cotton fabric strip right sides together along the longest edge. Stitch using a ¼in (6mm) seam allowance and cut off the excess. Turn the other long edge of the binding under ¼in (6mm), then turn to the wrong side of the patch and slip stitch to enclose the edge.

3. Use the excess to bind the other sides, turning the short edges under.

4. Pin to your item of clothing and stitch into place.

How to make the **gingham bag**

1. Cut your stitched fabric into a 6x6in (15x15cm) square with the initial placed centrally.

2. Cut the gingham into the following pieces: 6x16in (15x41cm), sides outer and 6x21in (15x53cm), sides lining. Two pieces 6x6in (15x15cm), base outer and lining. Two pieces 2½x12in (6x30cm), handles.

3. Use a ½in (1½cm) seam allowance and press all seams open as you go.

4. Place the side outer and the stitched Hardanger right sides together along one short end and stitch. Repeat to make a continuous loop.

5. Place the fabric base on top of the batting square and stitch it right sides together to the sides outer along all four sides.

6. Stitch the two short ends of the lining sides together, then stitch to the lining base in the same way as the outer.

7. Take one bag handle and fold it in half lengthways right sides together and stitch along the length. Turn right sides out and press. Repeat to make the other bag handle.

8. Pin one of the bag handles to the top of the front of the bag in order to position them at the corners of the bag top and matching raw edges. Pin the other handle to the back of the bag in the same place.

9. Now place the bag outer and bag lining right sides together by turning the lining inside out and placing the bag outer inside it. Stitch together around the top, enclosing the handles, and leave a 3in (8cm) opening along one side.

10. Turn right sides out, press and stitch along the top of the bag close to the edge to neaten, and stitch the opening close to complete.

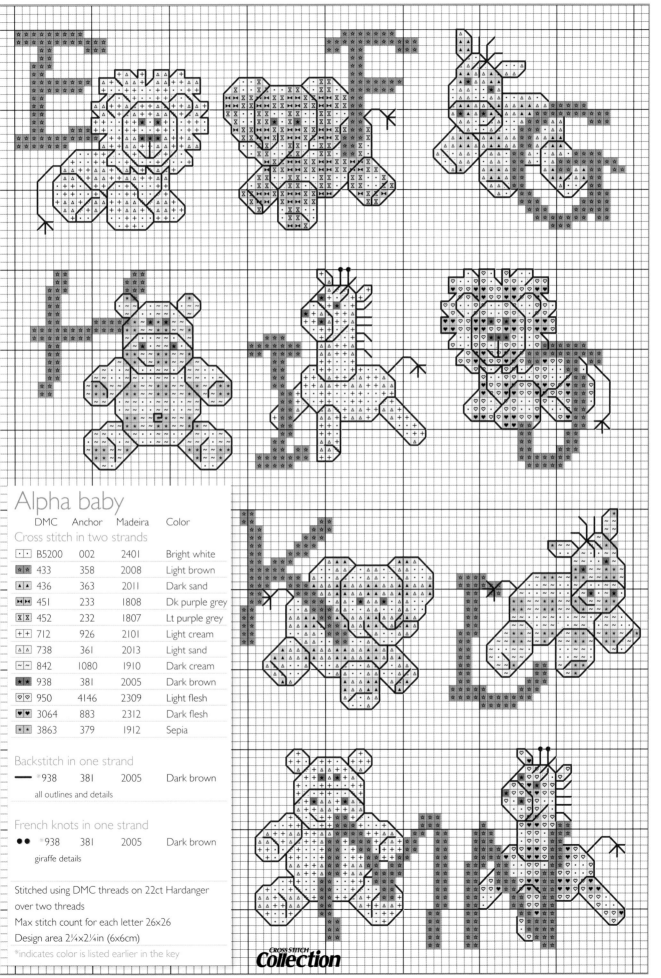

Alpha baby

	DMC	Anchor	Madeira	Color
Cross stitch in two strands				
·|·	B5200	002	2401	Bright white
☆|☆	433	358	2008	Light brown
▲|▲	436	363	2011	Dark sand
◄|◄	451	233	1808	Dk purple grey
☒|☒	452	232	1807	Lt purple grey
+|+	712	926	2101	Light cream
△|△	738	361	2013	Light sand
~|~	842	1080	1910	Dark cream
★|★	938	381	2005	Dark brown
♡|♡	950	4146	2309	Light flesh
♥|♥	3064	883	2312	Dark flesh
⊡|⊡	3863	379	1912	Sepia

Backstitch in one strand

——	*938	381	2005	Dark brown

all outlines and details

French knots in one strand

●●	*938	381	2005	Dark brown

giraffe details

Stitched using DMC threads on 22ct Hardanger
over two threads
Max stitch count for each letter 26x26
Design area 2¼x2¼in (6x6cm)
*indicates color is listed earlier in the key

CROSS STITCH
Collection

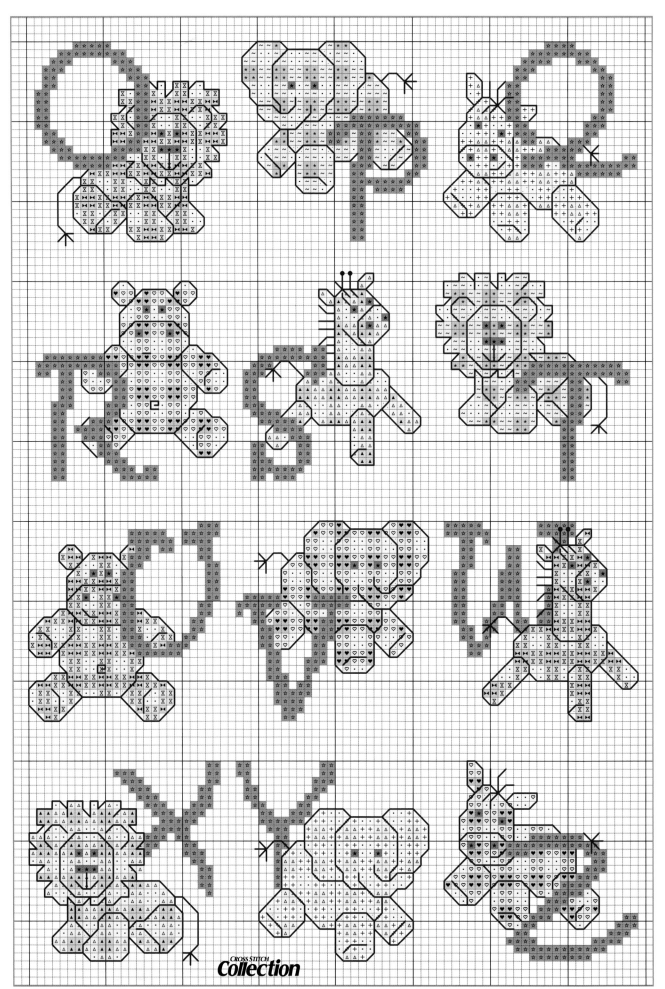

Art

With strong influences from the Arts & Crafts movement and Renaissance paintings, Maria brings artists' masterpieces to life

Subtle variations of sepia threads in ten different shades are all that is needed to create 'La Scapigliata', with backstitch adding the final touches

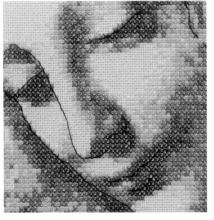 

Leonardo DaVinci's
La Scapigliata

Create your very own cross stitch masterpiece by making Leonardo da Vinci's painting appear on your canvas

This woman's head, known as 'La Scapigliata' (the uncombed or tousled) was painted by da Vinci circa 1508 and now resides at the Galleria Nazionale in Parma, Italy. Capturing the essence of a painting in cross stitch is notoriously difficult, but Maria has done a wonderful job with this piece, superbly portraying the tranquil grace and beauty of the original—and all using just nine shades of thread! Maria particularly enjoyed the challenge of this piece, "These sepia designs are a bit of a secret love of mine. Studying art, I was always particularly interested in preliminary drawings; they exhibit a freedom and honesty that is sometimes lost in the final paintings."

Only six shades of thread are used for the cross stitch and one shade for backstitch, so you can easily keep all of them threaded up and to hand at once

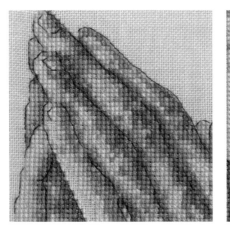

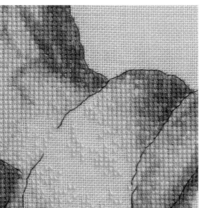

Praying hands

Based on a work by Albrecht Dürer, these hands clasped together in prayer are a truly iconic image

Dürer was a multi-talented artist, working as a painter, printmaker and engraver, but to our knowledge he never cross stitched, so this is a first for him! Maria has taken 'The Praying Hands' ('Betende Hände') and turned it into a sepia cross stitch that captures the essence of the piece beautifully on the Zweigart Cashel linen. The hands are actually a preparatory drawing by Dürer for the Heller Altarpiece, which was destroyed by fire in 1729. The original drawing was created in around the year 1508 in Vienna. ➤

➤ Getting organized

This design is fairly simple to stitch, in that there are no fractional stitches, and the whole design is worked in whole cross stitch with just a little backstitch. It is worked on a cream linen, so the background area is less prominent against the cross stitches. It is worked in six different shades of sepia embroidery floss, so you will have to make sure that you are stitching with the right color in the right place.

When you are stitching with several colors of similar shades that are all worked fairly close together, it's easier if you thread your needles first with the correct threads before you get started. Then, as you stitch, you can work a few stitches in one color and easily move on to the next without unthreading your needle. Simply take your threaded needle out to the front of the fabric near the edge and 'park' it by pushing it through the fabric. Now you can work the stitches in another color. This will save you lots of time finishing off threads or counting to work all the stitches in the same color at once. Also, by keeping the threads in the needle and attaching them to the fabric, the thread won't get tangled at the back.

Praying hands

DMC	Anchor	Madeira	Color
Cross stitch in two strands			
③③ 437	362	2012	Tan
⋈⋈ 632	936	2311	Dark sepia
⊡⊡ 738	361	2013	Dark cream
⊡⊡ 739	366	2014	Light cream
@@ 3064	1008	2312	Light sepia
#|# 3772	1007	2601	Medium sepia
Backstitch in one strand			
— 838	1088	2005	Brown
all outlines and details			

Stitched using DMC threads on 28ct linen over two threads
Stitch count 132×105
Design area 9½×7½in (24×19cm)

Cross stitch... **gadgets**

If you like gadgets then this project is a perfect excuse to add another one to your cross stitching equipment. A needle organizer is a gadget that keeps all your threaded needles in place with cards to write on the color names, numbers and chart symbols. It's just like a thread organizer, but will hold your threaded needles instead. You can find them at good needlework shops, or they can easily be bought by mail order or online. Needle organizers are also excellent for people who struggle to thread their needles. You can thread them all up in good daylight for evening stitching.

Working the cross stitch

Fold the fabric in half both ways to find the center and start stitching at this point. All the cross stitch is worked in two strands over two threads of the linen. As the embroidery floss colors are very close in shade, it's important to keep counting and re-counting. You will find it a lot easier if you cross off the stitches you have worked on the chart with a fluorescent pen as you go. For designs like this one, extra counting saves unpicking later on.

Adding the details

The details on the design are added when you have finished all of the cross stitch. All the backstitch is worked in one strand of Brown embroidery floss.

Renaissance **artist Bernardino Luini's 16th century style has been perfectly captured in this cross stitch design, cleverly using backstitch for the light and shade detail**

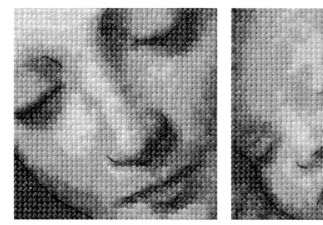

Madonna & child

Create your very own biblical scene by cross stitching this serene interpretation of an Italian Renaissance masterpiece

Now and again you come across a design that stops you in your tracks and makes you go, "Wow!" And this beautiful 'Madonna And Child' design—inspired by Bernardino Luini's painting, 'Infant Asleep'—certainly has the 'wow!' factor! Maria explains that she was drawn to the painting, not because of its history, but simply because she is a mom. "Oh, I love this painting! Can't you just tell I am a mother of boys? There is nothing lovelier than them falling asleep while you're cuddling them and it is the only time they actually sit still enough for a snuggle these days!" ➤

125

Shopping list...

- ✦ 16ct aida, 15x17in (38x43cm) white (or 32ct evenweave)
- ✦ Embroidery floss, as listed in the key
- ✦ Frame, with a 7x8¾in (18x22cm) aperture, antique gilt

Changing the colors tip

As there are only nine colors used it's very simple to change them as you wish. The best way to do this is with a shade card. Look closely at all the shades used, then match them in tonal value as closely as possible to the colorway you want to use. You could stitch it in black and white for a crisper effect. As the design is of a mother and baby, it would make the perfect gift for a new mother, or to hang in the nursery, so you could stitch it in shades of pink or blue for a very unique picture.

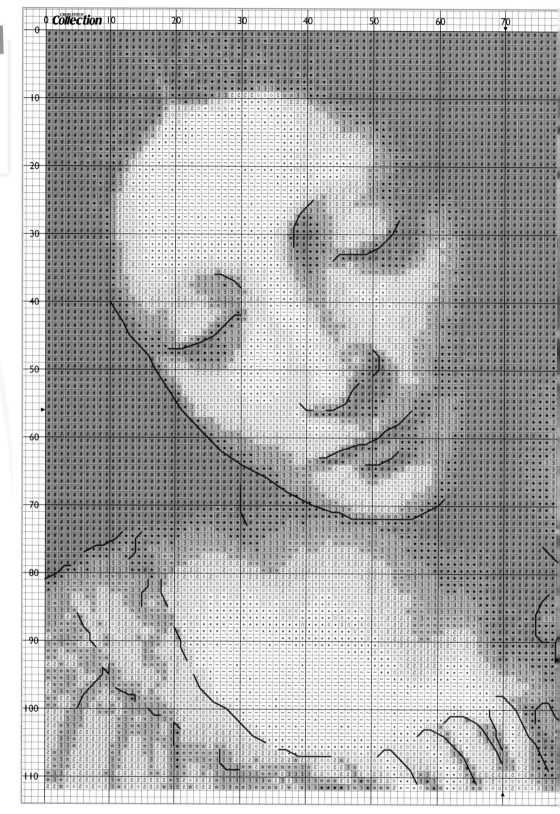

Working on... 16ct

This design has been worked on 16ct aida because it's solidly stitched and therefore it's very important that the white fabric doesn't show though the brown background stitching. You get a much better thread coverage on 16ct than 14ct for a design like this.

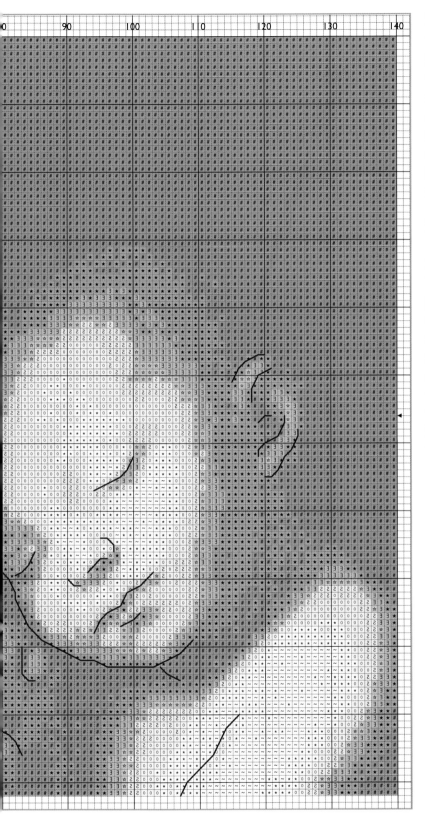

➤ Getting organized

There are only nine different colors of thread used in this design but they are all very similar in color. With this in mind, it's worth making a small thread organizer to keep them all labeled separately so you don't get them confused as you stitch. If you look at the key, you will see that you need to buy three skeins of Light brown, which is used to work the background. Three skeins might seem like a lot, but there is actually quite a lot of background to stitch.

Stitching the design

Fold the fabric in half both ways to find the center. This is the best place to start stitching to ensure you place your design correctly on the fabric. You will find it easier to stitch correctly if you work the two figures first then fill in the light brown background around them. All the cross stitch is worked in two strands over one thread of the aida. When you have finished working all the cross stitch, you need to add the backstitch details to bring the design to life. The backstitch details are all worked using one strand of Dark brown.

Madonna & child

	DMC	Anchor	Madeira	Color
Cross stitch in two strands				
~|~	White	002	2402	White
2|2	437	362	2012	Dark tan
★|★	632	936	2311	Dark sepia
*|★	712	926	2101	Cream
o|o	738	361	2013	Light tan
#|#	839	1086	1913	Light brown (3)
☆|★	3064	883	2312	Light sepia
3|3	3772	1007	2310	Medium sepia

Backstitch in one strand				
——	838	1088	2005	Dark brown
	all outlines and details			

Stitched using DMC threads on 16HPI aida
Stitch count 112x140
Design area 7x8¾in (18x22cm)
(3) indicates more than one skein required

Cross Stitched Cards
for the Holidays
ISBN: 978-1-57421-380-5
DO3503 **$9.99**

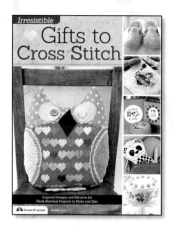

Irresistible Gifts to Cross Stitch
ISBN: 978-1-57421-445-1
DO5416 **$19.99**

Cross Stitched Cards for
Special Occasions
ISBN: 978-1-57421-376-8
DO3500 **$9.99**

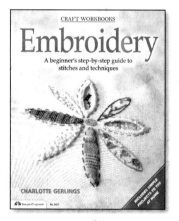

Embroidery
ISBN: 978-1-57421-500-7
DO5421 **$9.99**

Love Embroidery
ISBN: 978-1-57421-612-7
DO5302 **$17.99**

Sewing Pretty Little Things
ISBN: 978-1-57421-611-0
DO5301 **$19.99**

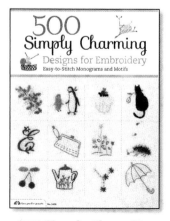

500 Simply Charming
Designs for Embroidery
ISBN: 978-1-57421-509-0
DO5430 **$14.99**

Felt from the Heart
ISBN: 978-1-57421-365-2
DO3488 **$9.99**

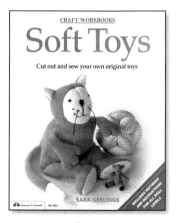

Soft Toys
ISBN: 978-1-57421-501-4
DO5422 **$9.99**